SO YOU THINK YOU'RE A NEW YORK METS FAN?

STARS, STATS, RECORDS, AND MEMORIES FOR TRUE DIEHARDS

BRETT TOPEL

SPORTS
PUBLISHING

Dedicated to some of the biggest Mets fans I know:
OT, EP, JB, Sam, Brian, and—of course—my Mom and Dad.
It is, after all, in my blood.

Sports Publishing books may be purchased in bulk at special discounts for sales promotion, corporate gifts, fund-raising, or educational purposes. Special editions can also be created to specifications. For details, contact the Special Sales Department, Sports Publishing, 307 West 36th Street, 11th Floor, New York, NY 10018 or sportspubbooks@skyhorsepublishing.com.

Sports Publishing® is a registered trademark of Skyhorse Publishing, Inc.®, a Delaware corporation.

Visit our website at www.sportspubbooks.com.

10 9 8 7 6 5 4 3 2 1

Library of Congress Cataloging-in-Publication Data is available on file.

Cover design by Tom Lau
Cover photo: Associated Press

ISBN: 978-1-61321-989-8
Ebook ISBN: 978-1-61321-990-4

Printed in the United States of America

Contents

ADVANCE PRAISE FOR
SO YOU THINK YOU'RE A NEW YORK METS FAN?

"Brett does an incredible job taking even the most ardent Mets fan down memory lane. I loved reading about the history of the club as told through various players' careers. The questions were awesome and will make great conversation! For me it's a must have for the serious Mets fan."
—Howard Johnson, All-Star third baseman

"This book is sure to challenge even the most knowledgeable Mets fan! It spans the six decades of the franchise's history, ensuring that there is something for everyone. It's a great read and a lot of fun."
—Doug Flynn, Gold Glove second baseman

INTRODUCTION

Sports fans and trivia go together as well as just about any analogy you can think of. Sports is about names, numbers, games, seasons, stats, and—most importantly—history. For diehards, it is a badge of honor to be able to stump your buddy, your mom or dad, or the guy you're sitting next to at a ballgame.

Mets fans, of course, are no different. There have been trivia books about the blue and orange in the past, each with its own set of challenging questions. However, this book will hopefully take Mets trivia to the next level. It's not always just about the question and the answer for the true fan, but the story behind the answer. How it happened, why it happened, and—sometimes most importantly—can it happen again? We all remember the big games and big names, but we need trivia questions to keep ourselves sharp when it comes to our team.

I once had someone question my status as a true Mets fan, asking me who the pitchers were for the 1969 world championship team, which by the way was one year before I was born. He said something like, "I know you will know Seaver and Koosman, everyone knows them, but who were the others?" As he looked at me, almost gleefully, I was careful not to take even a deep breath. I didn't want him to think I really needed to give it much thought. When I immediately replied, "Gary Gentry was their number three and Don Cardwell and Jim McAndrew rounded out the rotation," he looked stunned. He then said to me, "Ha, but you forgot Jon Matlack." I said, "Ha, no I didn't," knowing full well Matlack did not arrive to the Mets until 1971 and was actually part of the 1973 pennant winner. So be wary of those "know-it-all" fans who might ask questions that they themselves don't know the answers to! Turns out, that guy was a Yankees fan—different team, different book.

The Mets have one of the strongest fan bases in all of sports and they take their baseball—and their knowledge about their team—very seriously.

Former infielder Doug Flynn, who came to the Mets in the most controversial trade in franchise history—the deal that sent future Hall of Famer Tom Seaver to Cincinnati for four young players—summed up Mets fans very well: "If you keep your mouth shut, play hard, and own up to your mistakes, you won't have any trouble with Mets fans. They are purists of the game."

Because the Mets have only been a team for fifty-plus years, as opposed to a team like the New York Yankees, who have been around since 1903, their fans almost feel like they have been around for as long as the team itself. The truth his, however, that the Mets—having now been around for more than half a century—really do span generations. Younger Mets fans might not be able to handle the questions from the 1960s or 1970s or even the 1980s, but the nice thing about this book is that every era of Mets baseball is explored. The real hardcore fan will appreciate gaining new knowledge about the earlier teams.

While putting this book together, I was fortunate to speak to people who are close to the Mets, as well as some former players. The unique perspective they were able to give me really gives this book a lot of flavor and I am so thankful that they were willing to be involved with this project. One of my favorite interviews was with Doug Flynn, who I mentioned earlier. Despite coming to New York under very difficult circumstances, Flynn has terrific memories of his time here and of the friendships he made along the way. He shared an exchange he had with Pete Rose, his teammate in Cincinnati, who broke the news to him about the trade to the Mets just minutes after it happened:

"Two days before the trade, it was in the Cincinnati papers that I was untouchable and that I wasn't going any-where," said Flynn, who was a light-hitting, slick-fielding second baseman who, at the time, had played parts of only three seasons in the majors. "Someone had heard on the radio in the dugout that the trade had been made and they told Pete Rose, who was on the field. In between innings, Rose came into the dugout and sat down next to me."

"I looked at him and said, 'I'm gone?'," Flynn asked Rose.

"Yeah," Rose replied.

"Where am I going?"

"New York."

"Huh, which one?"

"You're going to the Mets."

"Really, who for?"

"Tom Seaver."

"Straight up?"

"Not hardly."

Luckily for Flynn, he was able to keep that sense of humor during his time in New York—a time when the Mets averaged ninety-seven losses a year. "I have great memories of my time in New York. We didn't win a whole lot, but I always appreciated Mets fans, and I was very fortunate to play in New York."

Whether you best-remember guys like Flynn and his teammates from the 1970s, the lovable—and then championship—Mets of the 1960s, the hard-nosed worst-to-first teams from the 1980s, the teams from the 1990s and 2000s, or the current crop of players, there are questions in this book for you. Not just your run-of-the-mill stat questions, but good, thought-provoking questions. There are questions that have answers right up through the end of the 2016 season, so this book is in not an out-of-date, historical account. All Mets fans know that when the Mets made the playoffs in 2016, it was only the second time in their history that the Mets made the postseason in back-to-back seasons. Well, you should know that! But what if you were asked to name some of the most "colorful" Mets of all time? Guys like Vic Black, Andrew Brown, Shawn Green, Tim Redding, and Rick White? Not to mention Henry Blanco? OK, enough of this, let's get this thing going.

This book is divided into four sections—the Early Innings, which will be Rookie Level questions; the Middle Innings, which will be Veteran Level questions; the Late Innings, which will be All-Star Level questions; and finally, Extra Innings, which will have the Hall of Fame Level questions. These are really for the expert Mets fan. So have some fun, and if you don't know some of the answers, that's fine. Those will be the questions you use to stump your buddy. Now, let's Play Ball!

1

EARLY INNINGS

ROOKIE LEVEL

ROOKIE LEVEL

OK, rook, it's time to get started on this long journey of Mets trivia. In reality, since fans come from different generations, what is an easy question for one diehard might be a harder one for another. You may remember facts from the early years, but younger fans in your family might have the newer ones covered. So feel free to have fun with this book with fellow Mets fans. This is all good fun, though, so do your best. This first group of questions are the easiest.

1 Who was the first-ever batter for the Mets? *Answer on page 8.*

2 Match these Mets to their nickname. *Answer on page 10.*

1. Rusty Staub	A: The Stork
2. Noah Syndergaard	B: The Hammer
3. Edgardo Alfonzo	C: Thor
4. George Theodore	D: Le Grand Orange
5. John Milner	E: Fonzie

3 Who slugged his 99th career homer against Jacob deGrom and the Mets, and his 100th career homer as a member of the Mets in 2016? *Answer on page 12.*

4 Which Mets star pitcher holds the major-league record for making the most opening-day starts? *(Note: Not all of them came when he was a member of the Mets.) Answer on page 13.*

5 The Mets have won 100 or more games in a season three times. Name the seasons. *Answer on page 14.*

6 In 1997, the Mets and Yankees played against each other in a regular season game for the first time. The Mets defeated the reigning world champions by a score of 6–0. Who was the winning pitcher? *Answer on page 15.*

7 Who is the Mets' all-time leader in triples and stolen bases? *Answer on page 16.*

8 Which player never played third base for the Mets?
   a. Hubie Brooks
   b. Gary Carter
   c. Mackey Sasser
   d. Kevin Mitchell
   e. Rafael Santana

   Answer on page 19.

9 Three Mets have been members of the 30-30 club (30 home runs and 30 stolen bases in a single season). However, who is the only Mets player who accomplished that feat an amazing three times? *Answer on page 21.*

10 The cover of the Mets' 1969 official yearbook featured the disembodied heads of Tom Seaver, Jerry

Koosman, and their All-Star batterymate. Who was he? *Answer on page 27.*

11 Which two players hold the Mets' record for most extra-base hits in a single season? *Answer on page 28.*

12 The cover of the Mets' 1982 official yearbook featured the caricatures of which two men along with the headline: By George, We've Got It! *Answer on page 29.*

13 Who was the first Met to win a Silver Slugger award? *Answer on page 31.*

14 Which relief pitcher has appeared in the most games in Mets history? *Answer on page 32.*

15 When Tom Seaver was traded to the Cincinnati Reds in 1977, the Mets received pitcher Pat Zachry, second baseman Doug Flynn, outfielder Steven Henderson, and which outfield prospect? *Answer on page 33.*

16 What was the most lopsided shutout victory in the history of the franchise? *Answer on page 35.*

17 Who was on deck for the Mets when the ball squirted through Bill Buckner's legs in Game Six of the 1986 World Series? *Answer on page 37.*

18 Who made the final out in Johan Santana's no-hitter? *Answer on page 39.*

19 In the 1986 music video "Let's Go Mets Go," comedian Joe Piscopo appears in the Mets dugout treating the real-life Mets as bobblehead dolls. Piscopo

goes down the bench, tapping Howard Johnson, Bob Ojeda, Rick Aguilera, and Kevin Mitchell. But which one-time Mets All-Star gets up and tackles Piscopo when his head is tapped? *Answer on page 40.*

20 OK, you have *almost* completed the Rookie Level of our trivia and are *almost* ready to advance to the Veteran Level questions. As I said, though, *almost*. At the end of every chapter of this book, you will need to complete a two-part Name Those Mets question. For each of these, we will be looking for teammates. You will be given five clues. However, the fewer the clues you need, the bigger the Mets fan you really are. The format is similar to the old game show, *Name That Tune*, which ran on television from 1953 to 1959 and again from 1974 to 1981.

On *Name That Tune*, contestants were asked to name a song in the fewest number of piano notes, after being given verbal clues. Name Those Mets will be played in a similar fashion. You will be given five clues, however, you can attempt to answer the question as soon as you think you know it. In other words, if you only need four, or three, or even fewer clues, go ahead and Name Those Mets. Let's just see how big of a Mets fan you really are. Remember, we will end each chapter this way. It is how you can truly advance to the next level.

Since this is the end of your rookie season, we will start it off pretty easy. Don't expect the Name Those Mets questions in the next three chapters to be such gimmees.

Here we go, Name Those Mets! Remember, we are looking for teammates.

CLUE #1: We are both infielders who made our major-league debuts in 1974, but teamed up for the '86 Mets.

CLUE #2: If you add our uniform numbers together, you would come up with thirty-nine.

CLUE #3: We were both team leaders and well-respected members of the '86 championship team.

CLUE #4: One of us has our first name, and one of us has our last name—start with the letter "K."

CLUE #5: We both ended our careers with an American League team.

You probably didn't need all five of those clues. However, whether you did or didn't need all the clues, hopefully you are ready to give your answer and move on to Veteran Level.

Answer on page 42.

ROOKIE LEVEL— ANSWERS

1 On April 11, 1962, a brand new franchise—the New York Mets—took the field against the St. Louis Cardinals and starting pitcher Larry Jackson. Leading off the game for the Mets was center fielder Richie Ashburn—a future Hall of Famer.

Ashburn had been purchased during the offseason from the Chicago Cubs. Ashburn had spent the 1960 and 1961 seasons with the Cubs, but it was with the Philadelphia Phillies that Ashburn had carved out his Hall of Fame plaque.

From 1948 to 1959, Ashburn was a four-time All-Star outfielder. In 1958, Ashburn had 215 hits—including a league-leading 13 triples—and led the National League in batting average (.350), on-base percentage (.440), walks (97), and plate appearances (725).

By 1962, Ashburn had the name recognition that the Mets were looking for. He, along with Gil Hodges, was part of the the Mets' sales pitch.

On Opening Day in 1962, at St. Louis's Busch Stadium, Ashburn led off against Jackson in front of 16,147 fans. The result? Ashburn hit a fly ball to St. Louis center fielder Curt Flood and the Mets franchise was underway.

Richie Ashburn batted .306 and was an All-Star in 1962, his last season in the majors. *AP Photo.*

Ashburn finished the night going 1-for-5 and scoring a run in the Mets' 11–4 loss. For the season—the last of Ashburn's career—he batted .306 in 135 games and was named the team's Most Valuable Player as well as its first All-Star Game representative.

"I was voted the best player on the worst major-league team ever assembled," Ashburn jokingly told Joe Durso of *The New York Times*. "And I never knew quite how to take that, whether I was being complimented or not."

2 1–D, 2–C, 3–E, 4–A, 5–B
This multiple-choice question really spans all six decades of the Mets' existence.

Rusty Staub, who played for the Mets from 1972 to 1975 and then again from 1981 to 1985, got his "second" nickname of Le Grand Orange from the fans in Montreal, where he played before coming to the Mets for the first time. It's derivation, of course, could be seen the second he took off his baseball cap. The Montreal fans fell in love with Staub, not just for his playing ability, but because he took the time to learn French. His was hugely popular there—despite only playing north of the border for four seasons—and his uniform number 10 was retired by the Expos, who went on to become the Washington Nationals. Of course, Daniel Joseph Staub's most well-known nickname is Rusty.

Noah Syndergaard is the most recent Met of this group, of course. He received his nickname early on in his career because of his larger-than-life size and his flowing blond locks. The resemblance between the Mets' powerful arm and that of the superhero is actually uncanny. On certain days, Syndergaard even appears to have the brute strength of Thor, especially when his fastball hits 100-plus.

Mets ace Noah Syndergaard truly embodies the nickname, Thor.
Photo courtesy of the National Baseball Hall of Fame Library.

There's a really good chance that Edgardo Alfonzo has never seen an episode of *Happy Days* and may or may not know about the famous sitcom biker that was portrayed by actor Henry Winkler in the 1970s. No matter—Alfonzo's nickname of Fonzie was simply an organic result of his name. And for a short time in Flushing, the Mets' Fonzie was about as cool as a player could be. In 1999 and again in 2000, Alfonzo hit over .300 and had a total of 52 home runs and 202 runs batted in. In 1999, he won the Silver Slugger Award at second base in the National League with his .304 average, while in 2000 he was selected to his only All-Star game.

George Theodore is likely less known to younger Mets fans, but those who remember the 1970s' versions of the franchise certainly remember The Stork. Theodore was not a particularly good player, hitting just .219 during his two seasons with the Mets in 1973 and '74. He might be best known for two things—a zany personality and an outfield collision with teammate Don Hahn during which Theodore was badly injured. He got his nickname because he stood 6-foot-4, not all that tall by today's standards. Still, the Stork is very fondly remembered by Mets fans and indeed he was on hand in 2008 when the Mets closed down their beloved Shea Stadium.

Then, there was John Milner—simply known as The Hammer. Of course, Milner was no Hank Aaron, but he did grow up idolizing the slugger, and was more than happy to have a nickname played off of Hammerin' Hank. He did show power early on in his career with the Mets, but finished his career with just 131 homers.

3 The only thing that would have made this question and answer more poetic would be if James Loney's milestone clout had given Jacob deGrom a win. Instead, rotation mate Noah Syndergaard benefitted.

When the Mets acquired Loney in early 2016, they were desperate. Lucas Duda had gone down with a long-term back injury and there was no one on the roster suited to play every day over the long haul. So after trying players such as Eric Campbell at first base, the Mets made their move. It was low risk, and—as it turned out—high reward.

At the time the Mets came calling, Loney was playing well—but really rotting away—with the San Diego Padres' AAA affiliate in El Paso. He was hitting .342 and for the Mets, he was worth a flyer. Plus, all the Mets had to send the Padres was cash—and not a lot of it.

Less than a week later, Loney squared off against Mike Dunn of the Miami Marlins. With the game tied 2–2 in the top of the seventh, Wilmer Flores led off with a walk, bringing up the veteran hitter. Loney ripped a Dunn delivery deep into the right-field seats giving the Mets a 4–2 lead and—more importantly—giving Loney his milestone bomb.

Never a power hitter, Loney's smile as he approached home plate gave him away—being back in the majors was clearly a lot more fun than playing in El Paso.

4 Tom Seaver pitched in the major leagues for 20 seasons. He was the opening-day starter for his team in 16 of those seasons—an incredible honor. It is not hard to understand why. Seaver was always the ace, whether he was pitching for the Mets, or the Reds—the two teams he played for the longest.

Seaver's first opening day was not his rookie year. In 1967, Seaver actually started the second game of the season, lasting just 5 2/3 innings—and hitting two batters—in an eventual win against the Pittsburgh Pirates. Seaver's 16–13 record that season, however, was good enough to make him the opening-day starter in 1968. That was the beginning of ten straight opening-day starts for the man, appropriately enough, known as The Franchise. Seaver's record in those ten starts was six wins and no losses. The Mets won one of the four non-decisions for Seaver in those games.

Following his trade to the Cincinnati Reds, Seaver would start three of the next four seasons for the Reds—1978, 1979, and 1981. He returned to the Mets for the 1983 season and pitched the opener against the Philadelphia Phillies, for his fourteenth opening-day start. It seemed that Seaver would not get too many more opportunities to start a season, considering he was past his best years. However, there were still two more openers to go for Tom Terrific.

In his quest for 300 victories, Seaver—at the age of forty—began the 1985 season for the Chicago White Sox . . . and won. He received the same honor for the White Sox in 1986, giving him a record sixteen opening-day starts. Likely one of the lesser-known records that will never be matched.

5 In the Mets' first two seasons, they were only able to win a combined 91 games. So the thought of winning 100 games in a season was slightly less than a pipe dream for the Mets and their fans. However, 1969 was a season when many pipe dreams were answered—and the Mets won 100 ballgames. Slightly less likely than having a man walk on the moon, still, both events occurred in the same year. The 1969 Mets went on to parlay their 100–62 record into a National League East crown, and an eventual world championship.

It took seventeen more years—and a lot of lean seasons—for the Mets to top the century mark in wins once again. And once again it was en route to a World Series title that the 1986 Mets completed the regular season with a record of 108–54. So dominant were the Mets that the second-place Philadelphia Phillies finished 21 1/2 games behind New York. The last-place Pittsburgh Pirates? They finished 44 games behind the Mets. It wasn't quite the 60 1/2 games back by the 1962 Mets, but it did show the 1986 team's pure dominance over the division.

Then there was the season of what could have been for the Mets—1988. That team, still packed with many of the players from the 1986 team, with the notable additions of Kevin McReynolds and David Cone, finished the regular season with a record of 100–60. However, the Mets lost to the Los Angeles Dodgers—a team they had dominated during the regular season—in the National League Championship Series. Just like that, the 1988 season was over.

The Mets came close to the 100-win mark three more times, winning 97 times in 1999 and 2006, and 94 times in 2000. Each of those teams advanced to the postseason, with the 2000 team losing in the World Series.

6 In 1997, the Mets' starting staff was not made up of the likes of Seaver, Koosman, and Matlack. Instead, the rotation was made up of Rick Reed, Bobby Jones, Mark Clark, and a twenty-nine-year-old right-hander who seemingly was missing a vowel in his name. Missing vowel or not, Dave Mlicki got the call for the Mets in that historic game at Yankee Stadium in the Bronx. The date was June 16, and Mlicki only had to face the defending champs in front of 56,188 screaming fans.

Heading into the game, Mlicki had a complete understanding of what the rivalry was all about.

"I took a walk out to Monument Park before the game, just to try and get a sense of the stadium, and I tell you, I got goosebumps," Mlicki said of the second incarnation of Yankee Stadium. "When the schedule came out before the season started, that was a date I circled that I wanted to pitch."

And pitch he did. Mlicki threw a complete-game shutout against the Yankees that night, striking out eight along the way. The Mets, in turn, jumped on Yankees starter Andy Pettitte early and coasted to the win. It was a night Mlicki will always remember.

"We were absolutely the underdog and really weren't supposed to do anything. They were the defending champs," Mlicki said. "At the time, I knew that it was big, but I didn't know how big. In fact it didn't really hit me until days later, and it was such a cool feeling. It was just awesome."

7 When Jose Reyes burst on the scene in 2003, he showed glimpses of the type of player he was going to be. At the age of twenty, Reyes played in only 69 games as a rookie, but batted over .300 and stole 13 bases. In his second season, detoured by injuries and a trip to second base—thank you, Kaz Matsui—Reyes was limited to only 53 games. By 2005, however, Reyes was ready to take on National League pitchers—and catchers.

Reyes led the league with 733 plate appearances, 696 at-bats, 17 triples, and 60 stolen bases in '05. He also had 190 hits and scored 99 runs. It was now very clear—Jose Reyes had arrived.

"He was the fastest Met I have ever seen," said Mets broadcaster Howie Rose, referring to the first time Reyes was called up. "In one of his first games, he tripled and I never saw a Met go from home to third as quickly as Reyes did. Before long, it became evident that he had this infectious enthusiasm that was going to play very well in New York and in that clubhouse."

The following year, as the Mets were marching toward a National League Eastern Division crown, Reyes led the league with 17 triples. His .300 batting average, 19 homers, and 81 runs batted in propelled Reyes to an All-Star appearance, a Silver Slugger Award, and a seventh-place finish in the Most Valuable Player voting. Oh yeah, he also led the National League during that 2006 season with 64 stolen bases.

After legging out 12 triples and an NL-best 78 steals in 2007—another All-Star season for the shortstop—Reyes had his most prolific year collecting three-base hits in 2008. In a season when he led the National League with 204 hits and had his third straight year of scoring more than 100 runs, Reyes stroked 19 triples in '08—the most he ever had during his career. Three seasons later, in the final year of his first stint with the Mets, Reyes ripped a league-leading 16 triples on his way to the National League batting title.

So the answer to who has the most triples and stolen bases for the Mets is, as you have figured by now, Jose Reyes. The question that remains is, how many will he end up with? After being reacquired by the Mets during

Jose Reyes led the National League in multiple offensive categories in 2005. *Photo courtesy of the National Baseball Hall of Fame Library.*

the summer of 2016, Reyes should have a lot more triples and stolen bases in him. Each time the four-time All-Star swipes a base or legs out a triple, he adds to his records. And as long as Jose is a member of the Mets, there is little doubt that he will be on the run!

8 If you answered that it was Mackey Sasser—seemingly the least likely player on the list to have played third base— unfortunately you are wrong. Sasser, the former backup and, at times, starting catcher for the Mets—who tended to get very hot at the plate, but had trouble throwing the ball back to the mound after pitches—actually did play third base for the Mets. It happened only twice—once in 1988 and once in 1989—each time lasting only two innings. However, that is enough to make Sasser a member of the long list of Mets third basemen.

"I had played shortstop in college and when they called me up, I had worked out at third and first and some in the outfield," Sasser said. "It came down to a situation where we had to make changes and double switches and I ended up playing in each of those games at third for a couple of innings. I had the chance to play third in some intrasquad games during spring training and it was great to be out there [during the regular season]. I didn't have any balls hit to me, but I wish I had. It was different for me, but it was a great opportunity because they had enough faith in me to put me out there at third base."

Sasser, who hit .307 in 1990 with the Mets, has great memories of playing in New York, despite the fact he is often remembered for having trouble throwing the ball back to the mound toward the end of his time with the Mets.

"I will always treasure the moments I got to play for New York," Sasser said. "I got to play in a big city where people love baseball and it was just a pleasure to be able to play for them. It was a great opportunity for me and I can always say that I did it in New York. That's a great feeling."

So if the answer isn't Mackey Sasser, it has to be the man he served as a backup for—Gary Carter, right? I mean, Carter was a Hall of Famer behind the plate, but why would he ever play third base? Well, Carter is not the answer, as he did play third base. Not only that, but in seasons when Carter played a game at third base, good things happened for the Mets. He played one game at third in 1986 (replacing Ray Knight, who had been ejected following an extra-inning brawl in Cincinnati)—clearly propelling the Mets to the world championship. He also played one game at third base in 1988, when the Mets advanced to the National League Championship Series.

OK, so it's not Sasser or Carter, as both catchers took a turn at the hot corner. Hubie Brooks is certainly not the answer, as Brooks was the Mets' starting third baseman for much of the early 1980s. In fact, Brooks had such a great season in 1984 that he played himself into being the key piece heading back to Montreal in the trade to acquire Gary Carter from the Expos. It was bittersweet for Mets fans, who had a great relationship with Brooks, who along with Mookie Wilson, became the faces of the young Mets after players like Lee Mazzilli were traded away. However, when you acquire Gary Carter, there is not too much to be bitter about. The Mets received one of the greatest players in all of baseball. For Brooks's part, his career took off in his first season in Montreal, driving in 100 runs for the only time. He went on to have an extremely solid 15-year career and even came back to the Mets for one season in 1991.

That leaves Kevin Mitchell and Rafael Santana. Santana played 483 games for the Mets over four seasons. He was a solid infielder and by far the quietest member of the 1986 championship team. Although he did let his hair down a bit in the "Let's Go Mets Go" music video, Santana was known mostly for his workmanlike approach to the game and his professionalism. His .248 batting average was perfectly fine on a team with so many stars and big bats. Santana was really like a silent partner, but the one you couldn't do without. Rafael Santana, however, never played third base for the Mets. He did play four games at third base for the St. Louis Cardinals in 1983, but never took the hot corner as a member of the Mets.

For the record, Kevin Mitchell played a total of 12 games at third base for the Mets in 1984 and 1986. During his career with the Mets, the slugging Mitchell played five of the nine positions—never catching, pitching, playing center field or second base.

9 Throughout the history of Major League Baseball, it had been among the rarest of feats—joining the "30-30 club." To enter this exclusive group, a player would need to combine great power with great speed, hitting at least thirty home runs and stealing at least thirty bases in the same season. That was not a combination that was found in too many players.

Prior to 1987, only five major league players—Ken Williams in 1922; Willie Mays in 1956 and '57; Hank Aaron in 1963; Tommy Harper in 1970; and Dale Murphy in 1983—had entered the elite group along with Bobby Bonds, who was not only a member of the club, he was the mayor. Bonds hit more than 30 home runs and stole more than 30 bases in the same season not once, nor twice, but FIVE times—in 1969, '73, '75, '77, and '78. (His son Barry would equal that incredible feat years later.)

In 1987, however, the locks were blown off of the doors to the 30-30 club, as four players joined the group in that one single season alone. It was the first season where more than one player reached those marks in the same year and two of those players were Mets—Darryl Strawberry and Howard Johnson.

Strawberry, one of the greatest sluggers in the game at that point, powered 39 homers and stole 36 bases. For all of his power and speed, however, 1987 was the only season that Strawberry would reach the 30–30 mark. He would come extremely close several other seasons, but would never again complete the mission.

Johnson, however, was just getting started in 1987. That season, the Mets infielder got the opportunity for the first time in his young career to play every day and Johnson did not disappoint. Playing mostly third base, HoJo slugged

36 home runs and drove in 99 runs. However, the most surprising aspect of Johnson's game ended up being his speed. Johnson stole 32 bases in 1987, gaining him entrance into the elite group.

"I remember going into the season, some of the writers were asking me what I was expecting to do as an everyday player," Johnson said. "I had told them that I thought I was going to hit twenty home runs and drive in eighty runs. However, I ended up getting to those numbers fairly quickly and I had a lot of games left in the season and I remember thinking, 'What is my goal going to be now?'"

At the time, the man that Mets fans called "HoJo" didn't know much about the exclusive milestone he was chasing.

"People were talking about 30–30, but I really had no idea what it was about," Johnson said. "I realized how rare it was because at that time very few players had ever done it.

So that became my goal, and sure enough I was able to accomplish it."

Unfortunately for Johnson, the day he entered the club was not a day that most Mets fans choose to remember. In fact, it was one of the most infamous in franchise history.

On September 11 of that year, The Mets and St. Louis Cardinals were battling for first place in the National League East and the homestanding Mets were leading 4–1 going into the ninth inning in front of more than 51,000 screaming fans at Shea. However, Roger McDowell would surrender a stunning home run to Terry Pendleton, and the Cards would go on to win that game—and eventually the division. All of a sudden, Johnson's amazing feat seemed to take a back seat.

"It was bittersweet," Johnson remembered. "It was kind of hollow when you accomplish something like that, but you lose such a big game like that. That could have been a really celebratory day for my teammates and me if we had won the game. So the day kind of ended up on a sour note."

After his numbers slipped to 24 home runs and 23 steals in 1988, Johnson had a terrific year in 1989, smacking 36 home runs and swiping 41 bases. For good measure, Johnson also poked 41 doubles, and led the National League with 109 runs scored. Johnson was elected to his first All-Star Game, won the Silver Slugger Award and finished fifth in the Most Valuable Player voting.

"Physically, I was coming into my prime that year and my body felt really strong," Johnson said. "I was finally healthy and feeling good. I got off to a good start and was able to put some numbers up."

Already an accomplished base stealer, in 1989 Johnson really worked on his technique, taking a tremendous amount of pride—not only in stealing over 40 bases, but being caught only eight times.

"I really tried to focus on being a really good base-stealer and someone with a good success rate," Johnson said. "I prided myself on being a guy who wasn't going to run just to run. I wanted to be safe every time I went. That was something I really worked on and tried to perfect—my jumps, my leads, knowing the pitchers, etcetera."

Following the 1989 season, Johnson felt as though he had finally made a statement to the rest of the league by joining the 30-30 club for the second time.

"I always told myself that you can do anything one time," Johnson said. "When you do it again, it really legitimizes it. It kind of proved, not only to myself, but also to the league that I was for real and that I was somebody that they had to pay attention to. It was really important for me to do it the second time. If they were going to pitch to me, then I was going to try and hurt them by hitting the ball somewhere hard and hit a home run or a double and if I had a chance to steal I was going to steal."

Johnson had possibly his finest offensive season for the Mets in 1991 when he made his third trip into the 30-30 club. Johnson led the National League with 38 home runs and 117 runs batted. He was selected to his second All-Star team, and once again won the Silver Slugger Award.

Still, Johnson was one stolen base shy of entering the 30-30 club for the third time as the Mets entered their 157th game of the season on October 1 against the Pittsburgh Pirates. In the top of the third inning, Johnson ripped a double down the third-base line to drive in the first run of the game. Johnson wasn't on second base for long. After teammate Kevin McReynolds was hit by a pitch, Johnson stole third base. Although HoJo was stranded on third, his swipe once again allowed him to regain entry into the 30-30 club.

"I remember I stole the base and I stood there and pulled the base out of the ground," Johnson said. "I told the umpire I was keeping the base. I just basically took it

Howard Johnson is the only player in Mets history to join the 30-30 club in three different seasons. *Photo courtesy of the National Baseball Hall of Fame Library.*

out of the ground and walked away with it into the dugout. It was kind of funny, I just picked it up and took it and I still have it."

Johnson is one of a handful of players in the game's history to accomplish that feat in three different seasons.

"To do it three times, I knew I was in elite company," Johnson said. "I am very proud of those seasons. It was an accomplishment that not a lot of guys can say they did and they can't take it away from you."

The third—and only other Mets player who gained membership into the club—is David Wright. In only his third full season with the Mets, Wright hit 30 home runs and stole 34 bases in 2007. Through the 2016 season, he is the last Met to enter the club.

10 The Mets have always been an organization known for having really good catchers. Whether it was one of the two Hall of Famers—Gary Carter and Mike Piazza—or the rugged John Stearns, Paul Lo Duca, or Todd Hundley—the Mets' field general has always been a big part of the team's success. That success dates back to their first star catcher—and the batterymate for the Mets' star arms of the 1960s and '70s—Jerry Grote.

"There's a synchronization that goes on between a pitcher and a catcher that keeps the game moving, keeps the tempo and keeps the flow," said Howie Rose. "When a catcher can think along with a pitcher about what they want to do in a certain spot to a certain hitter, it's a form of synchronization that allows for the maximum potential results."

Grote, who played for the Mets from 1966 to 1977, was the heart and soul of the Mets for more than a decade. The two-time All-Star behind the plate knew a thing or two about pitching as well, having been a pitcher himself in high school. In fact, he had a no-hitter on his résumé. However, the Mets were more than happy to have him on the other side of the dish, with arms like Seaver, Koosman, and Matlack, among many others. His arm was on display plenty of times, as he threw out more than 40 percent of the runners who tried to steal on him during his prime years. In his best defensive year, Grote threw out more than 50 percent of would-be stealers.

"He threw out Lou Brock seemingly with regularity and I am sure there were many good basestealers that he intimidated," Rose said. "From that standpoint alone, I was always in awe of how he controlled pretty good running games."

11 To be able to set a record such as most extra-base hits in a single season, a batter would most likely need to possess great power, but also have good speed to leg out doubles and triples. The two former Mets who are tied for this record were indeed blessed with both great power and speed. To start with, the record for most extra-base hits in a single season by a member of the Mets is 80.

The first person to reach the record was Howard Johnson, who in 1989 broke out with a tremendous offensive season. Johnson slugged 36 home runs, stroked a career-best 41 doubles, and legged out three triples. The fact that he also stole 41 bases that year was just gravy, and really has nothing to do with this answer, as impressive as it was.

"I got off to a good start and was able to put some numbers up that year," Johnson remembered. "To put those kind of numbers up for an entire season is very hard and it takes a lot out of you."

Johnson was rewarded for all of his hard work at the plate in 1989 when he received the Silver Slugger Award for being the best offensive third baseman in the National League.

For more than a decade, Johnson's mark of 80 extra-base hits stood as the most-ever by a member of the Mets. However, in 2006—as the Mets were chasing down a division title—Carlos Beltran equaled the mark.

That season, Beltran slugged 41 home runs, 38 doubles, and one triple. As Johnson did seventeen years earlier, Beltran also received the Silver Slugger Award.

Beltran added a little drama to his quest for tying the record, waiting until the sixth inning of game number 159 before hitting his 41st home run—which turned out to be his 80th extra-base hit.

12 The Mets were always fond of having mottos for each of their seasons. In 1983, they went with "Catch the Rising Stars" and in 1986, the championship season had been billed "Baseball Like it Oughta Be." However, prior to the Mets having rising stars and building a contender, the slogans—in retrospect—were a bit comical. The 1980 season, for example, had been billed as, "The Magic Is

Back." It was not really magical for Mets fans, however, who had to endure a 67–95 season. In 1981, the Mets tried again, promoting the year with, "The Magic Is Real." It wasn't. The Mets went on to a combined 41–62 in the strike-shortened season.

So nestled in between "The Magic Is Real" of 1981 and "Catch the Rising Stars" of 1983 was the transitional 1982 season. The Mets were not quite ready to contend for anything, but they had made some significant moves during the offseason. Two of those moves went by the name of George—new manager George Bamberger and former Cincinnati Reds slugger George Foster.

Bamberger took over the managerial reigns from Joe Torre, who had led the Mets through five of the darkest seasons in franchise history. Certainly, Bamberger would have to fare better. In 1978, Bamberger led the Milwaukee Brewers to a 93-win season and the following year led his team to a 95-win campaign. There was definitely a track record, despite the fact that he had resigned late the 1980 season after returning from a heart attack suffered during spring training that year.

For George Foster, 1982 was a much-needed change of scenery. He had spent the better part of the past eleven seasons with the Big Red Machine in Cincinnati. After crushing 52 and 40 home runs in successive seasons and leading the National League in runs batted in for the 1976, 1977, and 1978 seasons, Foster was still a force to be reckoned with in 1979, '80, and '81. In each of those years he drove in more than 90 runs and finished third in voting for the Most Valuable Player Award in 1981. The Mets were getting a bona fide star.

So when the cover of 1982's official yearbook shouted By George, We've Got It! the Mets' marketing staff must have been confident that the slogan was for real. History tells us another story, unfortunately.

Bamberger and the Mets went just 65–97 in 1982 and the Mets' new manager—depicted with his smiling face on the cover of the yearbook—was gone in May of his second season in New York.

Foster did not fare as badly as his first Mets manager, but his stay in New York was not all that memorable. Although the once-feared slugger continued to produce—albeit at a reduced rate than had been expected—he never lived up to the star the Mets thought they had traded for. Many forget that Foster was actually still on the Mets for nearly half of their magical run in 1986. After hitting just 13 home runs in 72 games, the Mets released George Foster in early August.

The cover of the 1982 yearbook, in the end, only lived up to the failed slogans of 1980 and 1981. There was no magic, by George.

13 It is a little bit of a loaded question asking who the first Met to win the Silver Slugger was because the award was not created until 1980. During that time, the Mets had few offensive players that were capable of leading the National League in hitting at their position. Then, things started to change.

The franchise started to turn around their fortunes in the early 1980s—young players such as Darryl Strawberry, Dwight Gooden, and Wally Backman were on the farm, and trades had been made for pitchers such as Ron Darling and Walt Terrell. Then, the Mets made a stunning trade to acquire a former Most Valuable Player and five-time Gold Glove winner Keith Hernandez. Oh, and by the way, Hernandez won the very first Silver Slugger ever handed out in 1980 with a .321 batting average.

Heading into 1984, Hernandez left spring training with a positive outlook on the upcoming season, his first full year in New York.

"Last year was unique and very unsettling," Hernandez told reporters. "Pressure is not the right word, but when you get traded you want to do well. Now I've gotten to know the guys. I'm completely adjusted and happy. It feels like I've been a Met for five years."

Pressure or not, Hernandez showed everyone what he was all about and that he was one of the National League's best hitters. He batted .311 on the season, with 15 homers and 94 runs batted in. That earned Hernandez his second career Silver Slugger—and the first in Mets history. His .311 batting average was the highest he would hit throughout his six and a half seasons in New York.

14 When you really unpack this question, John Franco is the only person who should own this record. Franco, who grew up in Brooklyn—the son of a New York City sanitation worker—rooted for the Mets as a child. In addition,

he is a product of St. John's University, and in almost every aspect was pure New York.

Franco started his career about as far from New York as you could get when it comes to baseball, when he was selected by the Los Angeles Dodgers in the 1981 amateur draft. Franco never made it to Los Angeles, however, making his major league debut with the Cincinnati Reds in 1984. In his six seasons in the Queen City—a precursor to his time in Queens—Franco averaged nearly 25 saves per season. However, his career would never be the same after being traded for Mets closer Randy Myers before the 1990 season.

Franco fit in perfectly at Shea Stadium, where he would go on to become a team leader and fan favorite. He helped propel the Mets into the postseason in 1999 and 2000—the first time in franchise history that the Mets made the playoffs in consecutive seasons. He was named team captain in 2001, a position he would hold for four seasons until he left the Mets.

Franco holds the team record for saves with 276, games finished with 484, and, yes, games pitched—with 695.

15 There is no transaction in Mets history that resonates as much negativity as the trade of Tom Seaver to the Cincinnati Reds during the 1977 season. Seaver was, after all, The Franchise. He had led the Mets to a world championship in 1969, a pennant in 1973, and was a three-time Cy Young Award winner. Not to mention up to the point in his career, he was a nine-time All-Star. However, the Mets were terrible and the team's top executive and Seaver did not get along. So the Mets made their worst-ever trade. Worse than Nolan Ryan for Jim Fregosi, worse than Rusty Staub for Mickey Lolich, worse than Scott Kazmir for Victor Zambrano.

In exchange for the pitcher who had stuck out more than 200 batters in nine of his first ten seasons with the Mets, New York received a handful of players that would never amount to much. Pat Zachry was an average starting pitcher for the Mets in the late 1970s and early 1980s; Doug Flynn did win a Gold Glove at second base in 1980; Steve Henderson had flashes of greatness, but was soon shipped out of town.

"My first day out on the field I heard this voice say, 'Mr. Flynn,'" the former infielder remembered. "I turned around and saw a very nice looking gentleman. I said, 'Hey, how you doing?' He said, '*You suck*!' I just started laughing."

Despite the rough treatment from some of the fans initially, Flynn was proud to talk about the reaction he and his Reds teammates that came over in the trade received from the Mets' players.

"We were treated so well by the players on that team," Flynn said. "I'm talking about guys like Koosy and Matlack and Grote and Buddy [Harrelson]. All of those guys treated us so well. They lost a dear teammate, but they knew that that was the nature of the game and that we had nothing to do with the trade. I have a lot of respect for the city, for the fans, and for the team, and certainly I feel very blessed that I had the chance to play there for four and a half years."

There was one more player in the deal, who most likely doesn't have those same good memories, as he is often forgotten completely. Outfielder Dan Norman was a top prospect for the Reds, but never appeared in a major league game for Cincinnati. He was eventually called up to the majors by the Mets for parts of the 1978 and 1979 seasons, but struggled each time he came up. Often injured, Norman remained in the majors for an entire season only once, in 1980. However, the outfielder hit below .200 and by 1981, he was packaged with pitcher Jeff Reardon and sent to the Montreal Expos for slugger Ellis Valentine. That, as it turned out, was also a bad trade for the Mets, as Reardon went on to be a premier relief pitcher for the Expos, leading the National League in saves in 1985. It's not often that one player is a part of two of the least successful trades in franchise history.

For Dan Norman—who was out of the majors by 1982—that was indeed the case.

16 Of all the answers to all the questions in this book, this one will be the most recent. That is because the answer to this question came in the last home game of the 2016 regular season.

One night earlier, with the Mets fighting for a wild-card spot, the Philadelphia Phillies jumped out to a 10–0 lead before all of the fans at Citi Field were even in their seats. The Mets scratched and clawed their way back into that game, only to lose by a score of 10–8.

The next day, however, the tables turned in a very big way. The Mets, with the assistance of a less-than-stellar Phillies' bullpen, went on to a 17–0 shutout victory. It was the largest shutout win in the team's history, surpassing two instances when the Mets had won 14–0.

After jumping out to a 3–0 lead after four innings, the Mets put up three more runs in the bottom of the fifth inning to take a 6–0 lead. New York then blew the game open in the bottom of the seventh when Asdrubal Cabrera's grand slam highlighted a five-run frame. Then, in the bottom of the eighth inning, the Mets added another six runs to make the final score 17–0. The Phillies—long out of any race—barely put up a fight. The Mets, it seemed, had nothing but fight.

"The guys have been really swinging the bat as a collective group and that means a lot," manager Terry Collins told reporters following the game. "We are not looking at just three or four guys."

Cabrera, in particular, became a fan favorite during the 2016 season, his first as a member of the Mets but his tenth in the big leagues. He played injured for much of the season, yet was one of the most reliable, clutch bats for the Mets throughout the season. He also set a team record for most home runs by a shortstop with 23, breaking the mark of his 2016 teammate Jose Reyes.

"With my experience, I think I've earned that respect from the team and from my teammates," Cabrera told reporters late in the season. "I always try to boost everyone's spirits."

Not lost in the offensive explosion against the Phillies was Robert Gsellman, who pitched the game of his young career to that point. The right-hander threw seven innings, gave up just three hits, walked only two batters, and struck out eight.

"I was working on my mechanics earlier in the week to fix some stuff and it seemed to work out today," Gsellman told reporters gathered around his locker following the game. "My curve ball was much sharper today. I am getting more confidence and want to keep it rolling."

17 Every Mets fan of a certain age has Mookie Wilson's "little roller up along first" burned in their memory banks. For fans of the orange and blue, it is one of those "I remember exactly where I was" moments. It was the final play, of the final inning, of the game simply remembered as "Game Six."

But what would have happened if Bill Buckner had not allowed Wilson's slow ground ball to get through his legs? Most people agree that Boston's hobbled first baseman was not going to beat the speedy Wilson to the bag. Most likely, Mookie would have been safe at first with an infield hit. However, under that scenario, the Mets would not have been able to end the game there. Ray Knight, who was on second base when the play began, would have gotten to third base, but certainly would not have scored on an infield hit. The Mets would have first and third with two outs—and the game would remain tied.

If the inning had played out that way, then who in fact would have been the next man to face the Red Sox? Interestingly enough, it would have been backup infielder Howard Johnson, who had been brought in earlier in the game to replace Kevin Elster at shortstop. Elster had come in to replace Rafael Santana, the team's starting shortstop. In fact, when the ball is seen going through Buckner's legs from the right-field camera, Johnson can be seen in the on-deck circle, leaping high into the air.

Johnson had already been the source of some controversy in Game Six—in fact, just one inning earlier. In the bottom of the ninth, with the score tied at three, Ray Knight led off the inning with a walk. Mookie Wilson laid down a bunt, but Boston catcher Rich Gedman committed a throwing error attempting to get Knight at second. When the dust cleared, the Mets had runners on first and second with nobody out. Johnson was then sent up to hit for Elster. Every single one of the fifty-five thousand–plus people at Shea Stadium knew what was coming. Johnson was going to bunt the runners to second and third. However, there was one thing that fans might not have been aware of that Mets manager Davey Johnson surely knew—HoJo had only one sacrifice bunt all season. Still, it was a no-brainer. That is what made it so confusing when Johnson did not bunt. Instead, he struck out. Perhaps, knowing how it turned out, Mets fans should be thankful that he did not bunt in that spot. Had he laid down a good one, the Mets may have won Game Six on a lazy sacrifice fly by Lee Mazzilli. Perhaps history needed Johnson to strike out.

Of course, after Johnson struck out, Mazzilli in fact did hit a lazy fly ball to left field for the second out, and Lenny Dykstra did the same. The ninth inning ended with the game tied—setting up inning number 10. The Mets sent enough batters to the plate in the bottom of the 10th inning with their game-tying rally to once again bring a turn at bat for Johnson—almost. In the end, it is an at-bat that Johnson was thrilled not to take.

18 When Johan Santana stepped onto the mound for the 8,020th game in New York Mets history on June 1, 2012, not one of the 27,069 fans in attendance could have realistically thought they were there to witness history. After all, it had been more than half a century, and despite having some of the top pitchers in baseball over the years, many believed that seeing a Mets no-hitter was never going to happen. Santana had pitched decently in the early part of the season, with a record of two wins and two losses. However, sometimes great things can happen when you least expect them. This was definitely one of those times.

Santana shut down the St. Louis Cardinals for the entire night, while the Mets beat up on St. Louis starter Adam Wainwright—a pitcher they were already holding a grudge against. Of course, it was Wainwright who froze Carlos Beltran to end the 2006 National League Championship Series. Ironically, Beltran was now a teammate of

Wainwright's. In fact, Beltran stroked the "foul ball" that will always be linked to Santana's no-hitter. But that has nothing to do with this question, which was who made the last out of the no-no?

While Santana did not surrender any hits throughout the first eight and two-third innings of the game, he did walk five batters. So with two outs in the ninth inning, Santana found himself staring at David Freese, the Cards' third baseman, sixty feet, six inches away. Freese worked a full count before Santana struck him out swinging to end the game. Finally, the impossible became reality for the Mets—and for Santana, who had never thrown a no-hitter in his life at any level of baseball.

"I don't think I've ever even thrown a no-hitter in video games," Santana told reporters after the game.

The historic nature of the event was not lost on Santana, who declined to take all of the credit for the milestone. He was thankful for the great defense played behind him—including a sparkling catch by left-fielder Mike Baxter—and the eight runs that the offense supported him with.

"We did this together," Santana told reporters after the game. "It is not just about me. We had a great, great game tonight. Everyone participated. We did the little things the way we were supposed to do it. And it worked out good. I thanked them because we as a team made history tonight."

19 So which player decided to take offense to Joe Piscopo—in a joking manner—of course? That would be Lee

Mazzilli, back for his second tour of duty with the Mets. From the time he reached the majors late in 1976 through the 1981 season, Mazzilli was the face of the Mets. His matinee-idol looks, combined with the fact that he was a Brooklyn guy, made him an absolute fan favorite. He was also, for much of his time in New York, the best player on the team. A career .259 hitter, Mazzilli hit as high as .303 for the Mets in 1979, the year he made the National League All-Star team.

"Lee was the face of the franchise in those years," said former Mets broadcaster Steve Albert. "Anytime you're a center fielder and a good player in New York, you're going to be in the spotlight."

The Mets traded Mazzilli before the 1982 season in exchange for pitching prospects Ron Darling and Walt Terrell. Mazzilli was not in Texas for long, however. In August of his first season, he was traded to the New York Yankees for shortstop Bucky Dent. Mazzilli played in just 37 games for the Yankees though, and was shipped to Pittsburgh following the season. In July of 1986, the Pirates released Mazzilli and the Mets immediately had interest, and signing him on August 3. In what was already a storybook season for the Mets, having their old star back in the fold to enjoy the run to a championship was a nice bonus for everyone.

"They say you can't go home, but I'm getting close," Mazzilli told *The New York Times* after signing with his former team.

Meanwhile, Mets general manager Frank Cashen was very pleased to have an old friend back. "We're delighted to have Maz back in the organization," Cashen told reporters. "He's going to Tidewater to play every day, something he hasn't been able to do in a couple of years. We feel that in time he's going to be back making a meaningful contribution to the Mets."

Cashen was indeed correct, as Mazzilli was a nice contributor for the Mets down the stretch and played in four of the seven World Series games. In the legendary Game Six, Mazzilli got the Mets' tying rally going with a single off of Calvin Schiraldi. He later tagged up on a Gary Carter fly ball to left that tied the score at three. Another pinch hit by Maz started a three-run rally in the bottom of the sixth inning of Game Seven. It was the only time during his 14-year career that Mazzilli would appear in a fall classic.

Twenty-five years after winning the World Series with the Mets, Mazzilli spoke of the victory at an awards dinner in upstate New York.

"It was a special team," he told the group. "It was a very confident team that had a lot of ability and great players, but most importantly they played as a team. That shows when you play together as a team, you win."

20 Are you able to Name Those Mets? Hopefully you can, because there are a lot more questions in this book and most of them are a lot harder than this one. The answer to the very first Name Those Mets is ... Keith Hernandez and Ray Knight.

Not only did Hernandez and Knight both come up in 1974, but they both played in only 14 games that first year. Hernandez came up with the St. Louis Cardinals as a twenty-year-old and went 10-for-34 (.294). It wouldn't be until 1979 that Hernandez would turn into the offensive player that he would come to be known as. During that season, he batted .344 with 48 doubles and shared Most Valuable Player honors in the National League. Knight, meanwhile, also came up in 1974—for the Cincinnati Reds. His career really got started three seasons later in 1977. Coincidentally, it was in 1979—much like Hernandez—that Knight broke out as a solid offensive player, batting .318—the highest he would ever hit.

As for uniform numbers, Hernandez—who wore number 37 for the Cardinals—had to make a change when he was traded to the Mets. In 1965, the Mets retired that number, which was worn by the franchise's first manager, Casey Stengel. So Hernandez went with number 17. Knight, meanwhile, wore number 25 throughout his career with the Reds. However, in 1981 he was traded to the Houston Astros and was forced to select a different number. In Houston, number 25 was being occupied by Jose Cruz, who was already a star with the Astros and was not going to give up his number. When Knight was traded to the Mets in 1984—one year after Hernandez arrived in Flushing—reserve outfielder Danny Heep had Knight's original number 25. Instead of going back to that number, however, Knight took his more recent number 22, which was being worn by coach Bobby Valentine, who switched to number 2.

As for the final clue on this question, you may remember that Keith Hernandez finished his career with one less-than-memorable season with the Cleveland Indians. Hernandez, who signed with Cleveland as a free agent before the 1989 season, appeared in just 43 games in 1990. That ended up being Hernandez's final season in the majors—one that he and his fans will most likely ignore. Knight, meanwhile, signed a free-agent contract with the Baltimore Orioles following the championship parade in 1986. He played for one season with the Orioles and then concluded his career in Detroit, playing one season for the Tigers.

2

MIDDLE INNINGS

VETERAN LEVEL

VETERAN LEVEL

Congratulations on making it to the Veteran Level. You are clearly smarter than the average Mets fan. But be warned, the questions get harder from here on out. If you know your stuff, you should be good to go. Remember, the two levels after this group of questions get even harder!

1 Which Mets pitcher was at one time an infielder at Stetson University? *Answer on page 51.*

2 The Mets won the World Series in 1969 and 1986. What did their two World Series MVPs have in common? *Answer on page 52.*

3 Which two Mets pitchers have won Silver Slugger Awards? *Answer on page 56.*

4 Name the only Mets pitchers to hit more than one home run in a single game. *Answer on page 57.*

5 When Tom Seaver made his return to the Mets on Opening Day in 1983, he struck out the game's leadoff hitter. Who was it? *Answer on page 59.*

6 Which Met holds the team record for most triples in a season with 21? *Answer on page 62.*

7 Rey-Rey-Rey: Over the 2002–2003 seasons, how did this name trifecta represent the Mets' shortstop situation? *Answer on page 62.*

8 What pitcher did Todd Pratt homer against in 1999 to send the Mets past the Arizona Diamondbacks and into the NLCS? *Answer on page 64.*

9 Who are the only two Mets to have a multi-homer game in the World Series? *Answer on page 65.*

10 Who was the first Met to drive in 100 runs for a season? *Answer on page 68.*

11 Who was the first Met to ever win a Gold Glove Award? *Answer on page 69.*

12 Which two members of the 1986 Mets appeared in the episode of *Seinfeld* entitled "The Boyfriend?" Bonus: A third player was mentioned. Who was he? *Answer on page 70.*

13 What future Hall of Famer threw seven brilliant innings out of the bullpen to earn the pennant-clinching victory in Game Three of the 1969 NLCS? *Answer on page 72.*

14 Who is the only second baseman to win a Gold Glove for the Mets? *Answer on page 73.*

15 What did year did the Mets share Shea Stadium with the New York Yankees, New York Jets, and New York Giants? *Answer on page 75.*

16 Which comedian, and longtime Mets fan, hit a home run at Citi Field during batting practice in 2016?

a. Jerry Seinfeld
b. Kevin James
c. Jim Breuer
d. Chris Rock

Answer on page 77.

17 Which three pitchers won a Cy Young Award as members of the Mets? *Answer on page 78.*

18 The Mets have had four team captains throughout their history. Name them. *Answer on page 80.*

19 For those who remember Shea Stadium well, you will recall that there were very few seats in the stadium itself—not counting the picnic area—that were in fair territory. In fact, only one player ever hit a home run into fair territory in the upper deck at Shea. Name him. *Answer on page 81.*

20 It's that time once again—the second edition of Name Those Mets! I am sure you remember the rules from the previous chapter. Basically, you are trying to name a pair of Mets teammates. As we move deeper into the book, Name Those Mets will continue to get harder. So this one is going to be a little harder than the last one, but probably a little easier to get than the two that will follow. OK, here we go, remember, try to use as few of the following clues as possible to name the pair of teammates.

CLUE #1: They were a battery for the Mets for nine seasons from the mid-1970s to the mid-1980s.

CLUE #2: The catcher was a four-time All-Star and the pitcher once led the National League in earned-run average.

CLUE #3: Injuries shortened both of these tremendously promising careers.

CLUE #4: The final season playing for the Mets for both men was 1984.

CLUE #5: While the Mets drafted the pitcher in the early 1970s, the catcher arrived when the Mets sent Tug McGraw and others to the Philadelphia Phillies.

OK, now it's all you—Name Those Mets!
Answer on page 83.

VETERAN LEVEL —
ANSWERS

1 In 2009, it wasn't a long shot that Jacob deGrom would be an All-Star pitcher in the major leagues—it was a no-shot. Following the 2009 season at Stetson College, deGrom's sophomore year, he was listed on the team roster simply as an infielder.

As a freshman, deGrom played 34 games, 28 of which he started at third base. DeGrom finished the season with just a .243 batting average. During his sophomore season, he started 36 of the 39 games he appeared in at shortstop. Still, his average improved to only .258.

In May of 2009, he made his first appearance as a pitcher for Stetson, coming on in relief. The following season, as a junior, he continued to play shortstop—mostly because he insisted—but was also being used as the team's closer because of his strong arm. It didn't take long before Stetson realized what it had in deGrom and he was taught how to throw a changeup and a slider to add to his blazing fastball.

The Mets took notice of deGrom and selected him in the ninth round of the 2010 amateur draft. He signed with the club and reported to Kingsport of the Appalachian League. He underwent Tommy John surgery that October.

After missing the 2011 season, deGrom worked his way up through the minors in 2012 and was promoted to the Mets in May of 2014. He made his major-league debut against the Yankees on May 15. In that interleague game, deGrom allowed one run over seven innings and his major-league career was underway, just a few years removed from shortstop at Stetson.

According to his coach at Stetson, the Mets' scouting of deGrom took a lot of outside-of-the-box thinking.

"[The Mets] knew they had a diamond in the rough," Pete Dunn told MLB.com. "As you can see now, they were 100 percent right."

2 To answer this question correctly, you first need to know who the two MVPs were, of course.

After spending eight seasons with the Pittsburgh Pirates, Donn Clendenon was left unprotected by Pittsburgh and was the eleventh pick by the Montreal Expos in the October 1968 expansion draft. However, it soon became clear that Clendenon might not have been destined to play north of the border. The following January, the Expos packaged Clendenon and Jesus Alou to the Houston Astros for Rusty Staub.

There was a problem with this entire situation, however. Houston had recently hired manager Harry Walker to lead their ballclub. Walker had managed Clendenon during part of his time in Pittsburgh, and the two had no love lost for each other. Clendenon refused to report to the Astros and announced his retirement.

His retirement was short-lived and—destiny or not—Clendenon ended up on the Expos' opening-day roster. After batting .240 with four homers and 14 RBIs in 38 games, the Expos traded the tall slugger to the second-place Mets for a bunch of minor leaguers. Because Rod Gaspar was wearing Clendenon's uniform number 17, the new Met was assigned number 22. Seemingly an unimportant detail.

Clendenon was only an average hitter with the Mets during the regular season, sharing playing time with Ed Kranepool at first base. In fact, after the Mets won the National League East, Clendenon did not appear in a single inning of the National League Championship Series. He was, however, saving his best for last.

In the 1969 World Series against the Baltimore Orioles, Clendenon's bat was on fire, hitting .357 with three home runs and four RBIs in the four games he played. That strong play earned the man, acquired by the Mets in June, World Series MVP honors.

"There is no most valuable player on this team—we've got lots of them," Clendenon told reporters after he was announced as the MVP. "It seems so strange to me when I didn't think I'd be playing ball at all this year. I had retired and I meant it." Luckily for the Mets, he hadn't.

It would take seventeen years before the Mets would have another World Series MVP. Unlike the 1969 Mets, the 1986 Mets were hardly a surprise to anyone. In fact, they were the overwhelming favorites to win it all. Following their 108-win regular season, the Mets went into the postseason as a confident bunch.

After the Houston Astros put a scare into the Mets in the NLCS, the Red Sox pushed them to virtual death. Only the legendary Mookie Wilson ground ball in Game Six, followed by a refuse-to-lose attitude in Game Seven, carried the Mets to their second World Series title.

Right in the middle of all of the action throughout the entirety of it all was third baseman Ray Knight. He was, in many ways, the heart of that 1986 Mets team. After going just 4-for-24 in the NLCS, Knight brought his good bats to the World Series. He batted .391 in the seven-game series, with a homer and five runs batted in. Of his nine hits, none was bigger than his two-out, two-strike flare to left-center in the bottom of the 10th inning of Game Six. He later rounded third and scored the winning run—with his hands on his helmet in disbelief—as he crossed the plate. Knight was mobbed in the Mets dugout, collapsing on the bench from pure exhaustion.

Following a home run and a Mets championship two nights later, Knight was named as the World Series MVP.

So, what did Clendenon and Knight have in common? They both wore uniform number 22.

Ray Knight will always be remembered for scoring the winning run in Game Six of the 1986 World Series. *Photo courtesy of the National Baseball Hall of Fame Library.*

3 The pitching-rich Mets franchise has had a number of terrific-hitting pitchers. However, only two of them have won the Silver Slugger Award, given to the best offensive player at each position.

An obvious answer would be someone like Tom Seaver, who was an excellent hitter. However, here's the rub—the Silver Slugger Award was given out for the first time in 1980. Seaver played for the Mets from 1967 to 1977 and then again in 1983. In 1971, Seaver actually flirted with a .200 batting average, finishing the year at .196 with a career-high 18 hits. However, again, there was no Silver Slugger in those days.

It took twelve years for a Mets pitcher to win a Silver Slugger, but in 1992—long after what most would consider his prime and the first year of his career that he was a sub-.500 pitcher—Dwight Gooden was a Silver Slugger. Gooden batted .264 on the season, collecting 19 hits. Included in those hits were a homer, three doubles, and one triple.

Eight seasons later, the Mets acquired one of the top pitchers—and top hitting pitchers—in all of baseball. In 1999, as a member of the Houston Astros, Mike Hampton went 22–4 with a 2.90 ERA. If that wasn't enough, he batted .311 with 23 hits and 10 runs batted in. Houston's ace easily cruised to his first Silver Slugger Award.

In the winter of 1999, the Astros traded Hampton to the Mets and he apparently packed all of his best bats. Hampton, who got off to a rough start on mound for the Mets, hardly struggled at the plate, batting .274 in his only season as a Met. He earned what would be his second of five straight Silver Slugger Awards.

Hampton added two more hits in the 2000 postseason for the Mets. Those didn't count towards the Silver Slugger, but they did help the Mets advance to the World Series.

4 It's happened twice. Still, it's hard to believe, given the fact that throughout their history of good hitting pitchers that only two of them have ever hit more than one homer in a game.

The first pitcher to accomplish the hitting feat not only clubbed two homers, but he did it in successive innings.

In August of 1983, the Mets were limping towards another 90-plus-loss season. While there were signs pointing towards a brighter future—which ended up being just one offseason away—the summer of 1983 had few highlights. One, however, was pitcher Walt Terrell's offensive outburst against the division rival Chicago Cubs.

Terrell had arrived to the Mets a year earlier, when he and fellow pitcher Ron Darling were acquired from the Texas Rangers for Lee Mazzilli. Although highly touted, Terrell did not provide the Mets much from the mound in his two-plus seasons in Flushing. He did, however, provide one special afternoon in 1983 at Wrigley Field.

What made the rookie pitcher's home-run binge even more impressive is the fact that he did it off of future Hall of Famer Fergie Jenkins. Sure, Jenkins was forty years old and in the final season of a brilliant career, but still—it was Fergie Jenkins.

In the top of the third inning, Terrell's batterymate, Ron Hodges, led off with a single to right field. Terrell then stepped up to the plate and sent a Jenkins pitch over the ivy-covered walls at Wrigley to give the Mets a 2–0 lead. Five more batters would come to the plate that inning, but the Mets did not score again in the frame.

That set up another Terrell at-bat in the very next inning. In the top of the fourth, with two men out and a runner on second base, Terrell did it again. His clout made him the first pitcher in the twenty-one-year history of the organization to hit two home runs in a game.

"It was just one of those things that happened, but I hope it happens some more," Terrell said after the game.

For the record, Terrell did homer one more time in 1983, giving him three on the year. He retired following the 1992 season with only those three career home runs.

Following the 1984 season, Terrell was traded to the Detroit Tigers straight-up for infielder Howard Johnson. That move worked out for both teams. Johnson, of course, went on to have a very solid career with the Mets and was a member of the 1986 world championship team. He was a member of the 30-30 club more than once and was a fan favorite.

Terrell, meanwhile, blossomed in Detroit, and had three very solid seasons as a starting pitcher before becoming a journeyman for the final five years of his career.

Twenty-three years later, the Mets were in a different position in the standings. They were no longer a perennial last-place team, but were, in fact, one of the favorites to make it to the World Series. Just one year earlier, in 2015, they had done just that, thanks in part to a rookie pitcher by the name of Noah Syndergaard.

Among Syndergaard's accomplishments in 2015 was pounding the first home run of his career. The man known as Thor doubled his 2015 home-run output in a single game against the Los Angeles Dodgers on May 11, 2016. In a battle of first-place teams, Syndergaard led off the top of the third inning against the Dodgers' Kenta Maeda. Thor ripped into the delivery and sent the ball over the right-center field fence to give the Mets a 1–0 lead.

After giving up a couple of home runs while on the mound, however, Syndergaard and the Mets found themselves trailing the Dodgers 2–1 as the game moved to the fifth inning.

In the top of the inning, the seventh- and eighth-place hitters both reached base, giving Syndergaard the chance to tie the game with a base hit. Instead, the power hitter bashed a low offering by Maeda over the left-center field fence for a three-run homer, giving the Mets a 4–2 lead and propelling him and the team to victory.

After the game, Syndergaard told reporters it was "a dream" and "an awesome experience."

5 Tom Seaver's first turn with the Mets ended badly for everyone—the fans, the players who were anointed to "replace" Seaver, and really for Seaver himself. Although the Reds were a better team than the Mets, they only advanced to the postseason once with Tom Terrific, losing in the National League Championship Series in 1979.

The Mets, meanwhile, fell into despair that few teams experience. From 1978 through 1982, they lost more than

90 games every season except 1981, which was a strike-plagued season. The players the Mets received for Seaver—Steve Henderson, Pat Zachry, Doug Flynn, and Dan Norman—were always labeled as being associated with that trade. The expectations were immense and unrealistic.

So when the Reds traded Seaver back to the Mets before the 1983 season, New York fans rejoiced. Sure, he was coming off a rough 1982 season (5–13 record with an ERA of 5.50), but having number 41 back meant something more than his performance on the mound.

On Opening Day in 1983 against the Philadelphia Phillies, the Mets fielded a starting lineup filled with a mix of young, promising players, older past-their-prime players, and players that never would be remembered for anything. However, on the mound in the center of Shea Stadium for the 1:35 p.m. start stood the man they called The Franchise. It was the very same mound from which he had led the Mets to the world title fourteen years earlier.

On this day, however, there would be no thoughts of titles. The Mets were going to be destined to lose more than 90 games again in 1983. But for that one moment, that one first batter, Seaver was back. The first batter he would face would be another superstar who was past his prime. In fact, the two had crossed paths, albeit briefly, in Cincinnati.

Leading off for the Phillies was the great Pete Rose. He wasn't there for long, however, as Seaver disposed of him quite handily, striking him out on a breaking ball.

Seaver scattered three hits over six innings that afternoon, giving up no runs and striking out five batters. The Mets won

Tom Seaver made a successful return to the mound at Shea on Opening Day in 1983. *Photo courtesy of the National Baseball Hall of Fame Library.*

the game, 2–0, but the runs were scored too late in the game for Seaver to get the win. That honor went to Doug Sisk. Seaver, meanwhile, would manage nine victories in 1983— the last year he would ever pitch for the Mets.

6 One thing was for certain about Lance Johnson—he could fly. His nickname was One Dog—not so much because of his speed, but because of the uniform number he wore. However, a more appropriate nickname might have been "Trips" or "3-Base" because Johnson was a master of triples. Arguably the hardest of all the hits to achieve, a triple has to combine a well-struck ball with blazing speed.

When Johnson came to the Mets in 1996, he had led the league in triples four of the five previous seasons. Over those five seasons as a member of the Chicago White Sox, Johnson stroked an incredible 65 triples. He was saving his best, however, for the big gaps of Shea Stadium.

Always known as a pitcher's park, Shea was also a haven for hitters who could find the deep gaps. In 1996, Johnson found them often—hitting a career-high and franchise-record 21 triples. Two players tied for second place behind Johnson. When their triples were added together, the number still fell short of Johnson's mark. Only Snuffy Stirnweiss (22 triples in 1945), Dale Mitchell (23 in 1949), and Curtis Granderson (23 in 2007) had more triples in a single season since the end of World War II.

7 The Mets' starting shortstop in 2002 was slick-fielding Rey Ordonez. It would be Ordonez's seventh and final season as a member of the Mets, but it was a short career that would be long remembered.

Ordonez came to the Mets for the 1996 season, after defecting from his native Cuba. He played almost every game at shortstop for the Mets that year, made some remarkable plays in the field, and received votes for Rookie of the Year honors in the National League. While he fell short of being named Rookie of the Year, there was hardware in Ordonez's near future. In 1997, 1998, and 1999, Ordonez was named as the Gold Glove Award winner. His defensive play at shortstop rivaled the best who had ever played the game. His patented sliding stop and throw to first base was being emulated by little leaguers on every sandlot in Queens. In 1999, Ordonez made just four errors in 640 chances, giving him an incredible fielding percentage of .994.

Following the 2002 season, the Mets traded Ordonez to the Tampa Bay Devil Rays. There was another Rey waiting in the wings—19-year-old Jose Reyes. During his first season, Reyes split time with yet another Rey—Rey Sanchez. Sanchez was a thirty-five-year-old who began the 2003 season as the Mets' starting shortstop. However, after he landed on the disabled list, Reyes was able to show what he could do. Unfortunately, an ankle injury cut short Reyes's first season. Still, it was clear that the Mets had a star young shortstop. That's what made what was about to happen even stranger.

Prior to the start of the 2004 season, the Mets signed Japanese shortstop Kaz Matsui, promising him he would be the team's starting shortstop. The Mets moved Reyes to second base to make room for the flashy import, who quickly looked like more of a flash in the pan. Reyes was hurt for much of the 2004 season, never seeing much action on the other side of the second-base bag. By the time Reyes got healthy for the start of the 2005 season, he was reinstated as the team's starting shortstop. Matsui was moved to second base.

Reyes quickly established himself as one of the top young shortstops in the game, and in 2005 became a star in New York and in the National League. During that season, the twenty-two-year-old led the league in plate appearances, at-bats, triples, and stolen bases. It was the first of three consecutive years that he would lead the league in stolen bases.

8 Todd Pratt might be the unlikeliest of heroes when you look at Mets postseason history. Sure, Ron Swoboda made a magical catch in right field in the 1969 World Series and Endy Chavez made a once-in-a-lifetime catch during the 2006 National League Championship Series—but no one tops Pratt in the hero department.

Throughout the entire regular season in 1999, Pratt appeared in just 71 games, with three homers and less than two dozen runs batted in. No one really cared, though. The Mets had Mike Piazza as their catcher. How often would his backup appear in games, anyway? By the time the regular season ended, however, Piazza was more than a little banged up—specifically nursing a bad thumb. After playing the first two games of the National League Division Series against the Arizona Diamondbacks, Piazza did not play in Game Three, and was spelled by Pratt, who did not get a hit. In fact, by the time Pratt came to bat in the bottom of the 10th inning of Game Four of the Series, Pratt had gone hitless in nine trips to the plate.

When the game headed into extra innings—and the Mets holding a two-games-to-one lead in the best-of-five series—the more than fifty-six thousand fans in attendance at Shea Stadium were hopeful that they would get to witness a dramatic walk-off, series-winning event.

After Robin Ventura flew out to right field for the first out of the tenth inning, Pratt strode to the plate to face Arizona reliever Matt Mantei. The rest, as they say, is history—the kind of thing that becomes an answer in a trivia book about a team. Pratt sent Mantei's delivery deep into dead center at Shea. Center fielder Steve Finley went back, back, back and leaped—well, did a short jump—attempting to make the catch. Finley didn't get very far off the ground, Pratt's deep fly eluded his glove and Shea Stadium exploded in happiness.

9 The 1986 Mets are remembered for a lot of things. The team won 108 games during the regular season, survived and prevailed in an absolutely terrific Game Six of the National League Championship Series against the Houston Astros, and—of course—went on to their memorable World Series victory over the Boston Red Sox. When fans think back to that World Series win, the first game that is always brought up is Game Six—and for good reason. However, if it had not been for Gary Carter's accomplishments in Game Three of that fall classic, it is unlikely that things would have gotten to Game Six.

The Mets had the honor of opening the 1986 World Series at Shea Stadium, playing host to the first two games. It was a great chance to jump on top of Boston and set the tone for the Series. What unfolded was exactly the opposite. The Red Sox took Game One by the slimmest of scores, 1–0. However, there was nothing slim about Game Two as the Red Sox blasted the Mets out of the building, pounding out nine runs on 18 hits and winning by a score of 9–3. The Mets were in trouble—big trouble—trailing the Red Sox two games to none and heading to Fenway Park for the next three games.

The 1986 Mets were nothing if they weren't resilient, though, and Lenny Dykstra led off Game Three by pulling a pitch from Boston's Dennis "Oil Can" Boyd over the right-field fence. In an instant, the Mets finally had a lead in the World Series. By the time the first inning was over, the Mets had scored four times to show that the Series was far from over. When Game Three came to an end, the Mets were 7–1 winners and trailed in the Series two games to one.

The Red Sox made one pretty big mistake apparently, before Game Three—they awoke a stumbling giant. They were overheard talking a little too confidently.

"The Sox were talking sweep," Gary Carter told reporters after the game. "We had won 112 games up to the World Series, and we knew we were better than to be swept."

The Mets would even the Series the next night, thanks to the offensive heroics—and first answer to this question—from Carter. With the game scoreless in the top of the fourth inning, Carter ripped an Al Nipper pitch over the Green Monster in left field for his first home run of the World Series. Four innings later, Carter did the exact same thing, this time off reliever Steve Crawford. With that blast, Carter ensured the Mets would be heading back to Shea Stadium, and became the first Mets player to ever hit two home runs in a World Series game. That mark stood for twenty-nine years—mostly because the Mets did not reach the World Series again until 2015.

When the Mets did surprise all of baseball and return to the fall classic in 2015, no one was a hotter hitter than Michael Conforto, the young outfielder who had started the season in Double-A Binghamton. In his 56 games with the Mets during the regular season, Conforto had hit nine home runs. He added another in the National League Division Series against the Los Angeles Dodgers. However, for the sake of this question, all that really matters is what Conforto did in Game Four of the World Series against the Kansas City Royals.

Down two games to one, the Mets were desperate to find some offense from anywhere. That offense came from Conforto, who led off the bottom of the third in a scoreless contest by ripping Chris Young's first pitch into the upper deck in right field. Just like that, the Mets had the lead. However, Conforto extended that lead when, in the bottom of the fifth inning, he blasted Danny Duffy's pitch over the right-center field wall. That home run matched Carter as the only members of the Mets to hit two home runs in a World Series game. Unfortunately for Conforto, his 2015 Mets were unable to hold that lead, as the Royals would win the game and the World Series. That, however, does not take away from the record-tying performance by Conforto.

10 Rusty Staub had a record-setting season at the plate in 1975. Now in his fourth season with the Mets, Staub was the team's best hitter. The right fielder batted close to .300 for much of the season, finishing the year with a .282 average. However, it was Staub's intelligence about the game and his clutch hitting that set him apart. For the first time in his 13-year career—and the first time in the

Rusty Staub, seen here during in the 1973 World Series, became the first Mets player to drive in 100 runs in a season two years later. *AP Photo.*

Mets' thirteen-year history—Staub drove in more than 100 runs, finishing 1975 with 105 runs batted in. He also had 30 doubles and 19 homers, which garnered him several votes in the Most Valuable Player voting at the end of the season.

The most runs ever driven in during a season by a member of the Mets was 124. That record is shared by Mike Piazza, who accomplished that feat in 1999, and David Wright, who matched it in 2008. In 2006, the year the Mets won the National League East, three players actually drove in more than 100 runs in the same season—Carlos Beltran (116), David Wright (116), and Carlos Delgado (114).

11 The Gold Glove Award has been the standard for fielders in Major League Baseball since 1957. To win one solidifies a defensive player's prowess forever. The Mets have won many Gold Gloves throughout their history, but the first did not come until after the franchise's ninth season—1970. That is when slick-fielding Tommie Agee—a player who had turned heads one year earlier by making two tremendous catches in the 1969 World Series—won the team's first-ever Gold Glove.

"People remember the two catches in the World Series, but it wasn't all like that, he was just a good, solid defender," said Howie Rose. "He wasn't flashy and he wasn't acrobatic, he was just stinking good. He's remembered for two of the most spectacular catches in the World Series, but he was a pretty graceful center fielder and I think that gets lost in the memories. Anything Tommie was going to get to, he was going to catch and it was a pleasure to watch him play."

Despite winning that Gold Glove, Agee really was a comet—streaking through for the Mets—rather than someone who had prolonged success with the team.

"His career as a successful Met was all too short, because you are really talking about just three years," Rose said. "Although one of those was the greatest of all Mets seasons—at least to me—the body of work just wasn't enough to sustain him to where you can say he had lasting power as one of the great all-time Mets."

12 "There had to be a second spitter . . . but who?"—one of the most classic lines from one of the most classic television sitcoms. *Seinfeld* was just coming into its own in 1992—season three for the show. On February 5 of that year, the show ventured into its first two-part episode. "The Boyfriend: Part 1" features the main character, Jerry Seinfeld, running into one of his heroes, Keith Hernandez, played by . . . wait for it . . . Keith Hernandez. The two strike up a quick friendship, while Keith falls for Jerry's ex-girlfriend, Elaine. As with every *Seinfeld* plot, there are several twists and turns in this episode, not the least of which is the fact that Kramer and Newman hate Hernandez because they claim he had spit on them after a game years earlier.

That sent the episode into a tribute, of sorts, to the movie *JFK*, which had been released around that time and featured the recurring line, "back and to the left" to describe Kennedy's head during his assassination. After hearing Kramer and Newman's explanation of the spitting event, Jerry keeps harping that Kramer's head had gone "back and to the left," proving that due to where Hernandez had been standing at the time, he could not have possibly spit on the pair. If it had been Hernandez, Seinfeld opines, it would have been "one magic loogie." No, instead, Seinfeld insists, there had to be a second spitter, behind the gravely road. But who?

It wasn't until the following week, on February 12, 1992, when "The Boyfriend: Part 2" aired, that Hernandez revealed that he had seen Roger McDowell lurking about the gravely road. "It was McDowell, but why?" Seinfeld asks. All of a sudden, Kramer and Newman remember that they had poured a beer on top of McDowell's head while they were in the stands and he was in the Mets bullpen. Instead of despising the former Mets first baseman, they decide to embrace him and actually go to help him move. But that is a whole other plot line.

Originally, according to reports, the second-spitter role had been written for Darryl Strawberry, but he was replaced because he was dealing with drug issues at the time. In 1997, *TV Guide* ranked "The Boyfriend" as the number-four show on its list of Top 100 all-time television episodes.

Now, for the bonus: There was one more member of the 1986 Mets that was mentioned in the episode, although he never appeared on camera. Do you remember who?

When Elaine returns to Jerry to describe her date with Hernandez, she blurts out excitedly, "Oh, Mookie... Mookie was there, do you know him?" So, Mookie Wilson became a footnote in the show's great history. One thing is clear, however: Mookie would never spit on anyone.

13 Game Three of the 1969 National League Championship Series certainly did not go as planned for Mets starter Gary Gentry. After the twenty-two-year-old rookie won 13 games for the Mets during the regular season, everyone had high hopes that Gentry would be the one to complete the three-game sweep over the Atlanta Braves. However, the Braves jumped on Gentry quickly, scoring two runs in the top of the first inning courtesy of Hank Aaron's two-run home run. That homer would be Aaron's last postseason homer, as Game Three was the final playoff game of Aaron's career.

Still, Gentry only lasted two-plus innings in the game. When manager Gil Hodges made his move to the bullpen, he brought in reliever Nolan Ryan. In a precursor to the Hall of Famer Ryan would become, the fireballer shut down the Braves for the next seven innings. The Braves, clearly, had no idea what they were in for.

"I didn't even know his name," Braves' cleanup hitter Rico Carty told reporters after the game, despite the fact that Ryan had played in parts of three seasons with the Mets at that point. "I never saw him before. It didn't make too much difference to me."

While Ryan did give up two earned runs when Orlando Cepeda smacked a two-run homer, he allowed little more. He gave up just two other hits and struck out seven batters in his seven innings. Unlike his teammate, Aaron knew exactly who Ryan was.

"Heck, we knew what he threw," Aaron told reporters after the game. "I've seen him in the past and he was erratic. He's nothing but a kid, but he did a helluva job out there."

14 The Mets have had several sure-handed second basemen throughout the franchise's history—guys like Felix Millan and Edgardo Alfonzo. However, it was Doug Flynn who won the only Gold Glove at second base as a Met. Flynn, who won the award in 1980, actually thought he had a better chance to win the award in one of his two previous seasons in New York.

"It really wasn't my best defensive year," Flynn said. "Maybe stat-wise it was, but I really thought I had a chance to win it in 1978 and 1979 because my stats were very comparative to the guys who won it. That was the time I realized it wasn't just about fielding percentage. But I really thought in 1979 when I led the league in assists, total chances, double plays, and putouts that I might have had a chance to get it, but I finished second."

Defense was always a priority for Flynn, who was not known as a particularly good offensive player.

"Playing defense was always very comfortable for me," Flynn said. "When I think back about my hitting,

Slick-fielding Doug Flynn is the only Mets second baseman to ever win a Gold Glove. *Photo courtesy of the National Baseball Hall of Fame Library.*

it was never anything I did that was worth a dime. If you go back to my high school team, I was probably hitting eighth on that team. It was just never comfortable for me, but playing defense was and I took a lot of pride in it. I worked at it and I tried to make myself better and, fortunately, I had a few skills there."

Flynn credits manager Joe Torre for playing him despite his lack of hitting.

"I owe so much to Joe because he gave me the opportunity to be in the lineup every day," Flynn said. "We were not playing very well, and struggling as a team, but he let me play every day when a lot of guys would not have, so I am very thankful to him for that."

As for the Gold Glove itself, Flynn still has it displayed prominently.

"I've got it at the house, drawing dust like everything else," Flynn joked. "It's still pretty neat when you think back. For a defensive player, it's really cool to win that award. When you don't win it, you think to yourself, 'OK, what do I need to do to get this?' It sits on my shelf very proudly. I was very thankful then, and I still am."

15 Read any good books lately? There was a really good one that came out in the spring of 2015 that was dedicated to this entire topic, in fact. I can't seem to remember who the author was, but the book was titled, *When Shea Was Home.* Oh yeah, I remember now, the author was me, and the full title was, *When Shea Was Home: The Story of the 1975 Mets, Yankees, Giants, and Jets.*

The story of the crazy 1975 season—when all four teams shared the one building in Flushing—was a result of Yankee Stadium being renovated. It was a little more complicated than that, of course, as the football Giants had announced in 1972—two years before the renovations—that they were going to move to New Jersey. The renovations that the City of New York had in store for the new Yankee Stadium did not suit the Giants' needs. It called for fewer seats, and that, along with other reasons, would not be acceptable for the proud football franchise. So the Giants left in 1973 and spent two seasons playing football at the Yale Bowl in Connecticut while waiting for their new home in New Jersey to be completed. That, in retrospect, was a mistake. So when new New York City Mayor Abraham Beame asked his buddy, Giants owner Wellington Mara, if he would like to play for one season at Shea Stadium, Mara relented. He didn't really want to do it, but he knew that he really didn't have a choice. The Giants had played miserably in Connecticut and his players hated it there. New Jersey was going to be their final destination, but a one-season stopover in Queens was in the cards for Big Blue.

The Yankees, meanwhile, were completing their second of two seasons at Shea Stadium while waiting for their new digs in the Bronx to be completed. Of course, the Jets had called Shea home since the stadium opened—and would do so until the 1984 season, when they fled to join the Giants in New Jersey.

The man who got the worst of it all—head groundskeeper Pete Flynn—was charged with keeping Shea Stadium playable for all of the teams.

"It was a nightmare," said Flynn, now retired and deservedly a member of the Major League Baseball

Groundskeepers Hall of Fame. "I didn't have a day off for months, and the field never got a day off. By the time the football season was over, there wasn't a blade of grass left in the entire place. That field just wasn't made to be used every day."

16 This one is not all that hard if you were paying attention to the 2016 season, as the King of Queens himself, Kevin James, was at just about every home game during the summer. Of course, James starred as Doug Heffernan—a die-hard Mets fan and delivery man living in Queens, on *The King of Queens* from 1998 to 2007. In the summer of 2016, James was promoting his new sitcom, *Kevin Can Wait*, where he plays a retired police officer who also just happens to be a, you guessed it, die-hard Mets fan. James—a Stony Brook native and Ward Melville High School graduate—really does bleed orange and blue.

In late September, James got the opportunity to take some cuts in the cage at Citi Field. Donning a number 7 jersey with the name "Kannon," sunglasses perched on top of his Mets cap, James crushed a pitch down the left-field line. As someone behind the cage shouted, "That's a walk-off!" James didn't budge, watching the flight of the ball. Only when it cleared the fence did the actor flip his bat high into the air and leap for the heavens, with both arms raised high. He then took his victorious journey around the bases. He was greeted at home plate with high-fives from several Mets players and coaches. After leaving the cage, James proudly stated, "There you go."

Following his big home run and during the actual game, James explained the depth of his Mets fandom with SNY reporter Steve Gelbs. "I've been a crazy Mets fan all my life," said James, whose daughter's name is Shea.

17 The Mets have had many Cy Young Award winners take the hill for them, but only three of those pitchers actually won the award as Mets. Those three hurlers accounted for a total of five Cy Young Awards, thanks mostly to Tom Seaver, who won the award three times.

Seaver's first Cy Young Award came following what many feel was the best of all Mets seasons, 1969. That year, Seaver won an incredible 25 games and lost only seven. While his earned-run average of 2.21 did not lead the National League, it was among the best in all of baseball. His performance led the Mets to 100 victories and the National League Eastern Division title, a National League pennant, and—oh, yeah, a world championship. Of course, none of the postseason accolades had anything to do with the Cy Young Award, which is voted on following the regular season. As an aside, Seaver finished just twenty-two votes behind Willie McCovey for National League Most Valuable Player honors. That is an award that no Mets player has ever won.

Seaver's second Cy Young Award came following the 1973 season, thanks to his 19 victories, his league-leading 18 complete games, league-leading 251 strikeouts, and league-best 2.08 earned-run average. For that season, Seaver was also best in the league in statistics that were not kept at the time, but have come to be respected by a new breed of baseball statisticians. Seaver's WHIP, which is walks plus hits divided by batters faced, would have been a National League–best 0.976. WAR is defined as the single number of wins that a player added to his team above what a replacement player would provide. On the WAR scale, a score of eight-plus is considered MVP-worthy. In 1973, Seaver's WAR would have been 11.0.

Seaver's third Cy Young Award came following the 1975 season, when he led the league with 22 victories and 243 strikeouts. This season marked the last season that Seaver would win as many as 22 games, but he did come close to winning a fourth Cy Young Award, finishing second in the voting in 1981 as a member of the Cincinnati Reds.

The second member of the Mets to win a Cy Young Award was Dwight Gooden, who in 1985—ten years after Seaver won his third award—had one of the greatest seasons any pitcher has ever had. That season, only Gooden's second in the big leagues, he led the National League in wins with 24, earned-run average with a mark of 1.53, complete games with 16, innings pitched with 276 2/3, and strikeouts with 268. Gooden's WAR, which like in the 1970s was not a stat that was kept, would have been an incredible 13.3. While pleased with his Cy Young, Gooden was more concerned that his team fell short of their goal of reaching the postseason.

"I'm honored to have my name listed with the other Cy Young winners," Gooden told reporters after winning the award. "Am I impressed by my numbers? Not really. The season was basically disappointing because we didn't win. We should have won. I think we should win next year." Of course, they would.

The third Mets pitcher to win the Cy Young was R.A. Dickey, who won the honor in 2012. Dickey, who came out of seemingly nowhere with his faster-than-usual knuckleball that had National League hitters reeling for three seasons, finally reached the top of the mountain, winning 20 games. Dickey led the National League with 230 strikeouts and five complete games. The thirty-seven-year-old became the first-ever knuckleballer to win the Cy Young.

18 The role of team captain in baseball is far less important than it is in other sports, such as hockey and football. In baseball, a team captain holds no real responsibility, but is really just a player that the other players have enough respect for that they are named captain. The Mets, in fact, did not even have a team captain until 1987 and that soon came under controversy.

In May of 1987, with the Mets struggling, manager Davey Johnson held a meeting with the team in which players were chastised about not being focused. However, there was more to the meeting, as Johnson wanted to do something to pay respect to the player who had been a team leader for the past several seasons, and at the same time perhaps spark the team—he named Keith Hernandez as the franchise's first-ever captain. Hernandez proudly had a "C" stitched into the front of his jersey. This was not actually commonplace for other teams to do, but the Mets have never been commonplace. In 1988, Gary Carter, who Johnson did not want to upset since Hernandez alone was named as the team captain one year earlier, was named co-captain. The pair reigned as captains through the 1989 season.

It wasn't until 2001 that the Mets named another team captain and that player was fan favorite John Franco. It was a title he would keep until he left the Mets after the 2004 season. Franco's popularity was not the lone reason for making him the captain, as he led the National League in saves for the Mets in 1990 and 1994.

Finally, the fourth captain of the Mets should have been an easy one to get, as he is the current captain of the team. David Wright, who came up with the Mets in 2004—and is one of their best-ever home-grown players—was named captain before the 2013 season.

"To be on that short list of guys that have been considered captain of this franchise is, for me, a dream come true, to say the least, and something that I'm very, very, very proud about," Wright told reporters following the announcement.

19 In April of 1969, no one had any idea how amazin' the Mets' season was truly going to be. However, if Tommie Agee's home run was a harbinger of things to come for that season, the sky was truly the limit. Man would walk on the moon later in the summer of 1969, but in

Tommie Agee's prolific blast was remembered by a marker in the upper deck at Shea Stadium. *Photo by alpineinc via Wikimedia Commons*.

April, Agee sent a ball into orbit, more than 480 feet from home plate. Here's the thing, though—it was an afternoon game that wasn't televised and there were only around eight thousand people in the ballpark. So there are not too many people who witnessed the mammoth blast. Still, it happened, and the home run was remembered forever when the organization painted a tribute to Agee where the ball landed, high into Section 48 of the upper deck. According to the Mets, the memorial was removed before Shea was torn down and sold to a private collector.

"I've never seen a ball hit like that," on-deck hitter Rod Gaspar said.

20 Were you able to Name Those Mets? They are John Stearns—the tough-nosed, fan-favorite catcher, and Craig Swan, the righty who always seemed to be ready to break out as a top pitcher. Unfortunately, Swan only showed glimpses of greatness, and was riddled with injuries for much of his career. He did, however, have a tremendous season statistically in 1978, winning the ERA title. In fact, at home his earned-run average was a stingy 1.68. However, those stats didn't translate to victories for Swan—or the Mets—who had one of the worst pitching staffs in baseball that season. Perhaps the highlight for Mets fans when it came to Swan was the fact that he appeared on the Topps baseball card in 1979 that depicted the ERA leaders from the previous season. On the card, Swan was pictured next to American League earned-run average leader, Ron Guidry of the Yankees. It was about the only parallel the Mets of the late 1970s had with the Yankees, who won back-to-back world championships in 1977 and 1978. That card became a source of pride for a generation of frustrated Mets fans. Beyond that, Swan is not often remembered.

Stearns was beset by injuries for his entire career. Still, he became an emotional leader and the starting catcher for the Mets in the late 1970s. While Swan was known best by a generation of Mets fans for one season record, Stearns was a four-time All-Star, often the lone representative from New York's National League squad.

3

LATE INNINGS

ALL-STAR LEVEL

ALL-STAR LEVEL

You are halfway there and it's now time for the All-Star Level. This one is not for lightweights. The questions in this level require more than knowing that the Mets have called three different buildings home, or that the scoreboard at Shea Stadium was the first one in history to be electronic. These questions require some thought and some real Mets thinking. Good luck!

1 When the Mets won the World Series in 1969 and 1986, the two pitchers who were on the mound when the final out was recorded were at one point traded for each other. Name the two pitchers. *Answer on page 92.*

2 What uniform number did Dwight Gooden wear during his first major league spring training with the Mets in 1984? *Answer on page 93.*

3 Which Mets slugger's mother played softball in the 2000 Olympics? *Answer on page 95.*

4 When Tom Seaver returned to the Mets in 1983, he shut down the Philadelphia Phillies for six innings, en route to a 2–0 victory. Seaver, however, did not get the win in the game. Who did? *Answer on page 97.*

5 The Mets have had the number one overall pick in the Major League Baseball amateur draft five times. Name their picks. *Answer on page 98.*

6 Who set the dubious major-league record of grounding into four double plays in a single game? *Answer on page 101.*

7 Which Met became the oldest major leaguer to hit the first home run of his career? *Answer on page 102.*

8 Who is the only player to hit his 500th home run as a member of the Mets? *Answer on page 104.*

9 In his first game as a Met, Gary Carter hit a walk-off home run against which one-time Mets reliever? *Answer on page 106.*

10 Which batter holds the team record for consecutive games with a home run during the regular season? *Answer on page 108.*

11 As every Mets fan knows, Johan Santana is the only pitcher to ever throw a no-hitter for the team. However, seven other pitchers who were once Mets have gone on to throw no-hitters with another team. Can you name them? *Answer on page 110.*

12 True or False: Shea Stadium was originally going to be designed with a retractable dome. *Answer on page 114.*

13 Which Mets catcher caught the most games without ever playing another position for the team? *Answer on page 115.*

14 From 1962 through 1978, the Mets had three broadcasters that shared television and radio responsibilities—Ralph Kiner, Bob Murphy, and Lindsey Nelson. Following the 1978 season, however, Nelson left the broadcast team. Who replaced him? *Answer on page 116.*

15 When the Mets traded David Cone to the Toronto Blue Jays in 1992, what two players did they receive in return? *Answer on page 118.*

16 Only three Mets first basemen have driven in 100 or more runs in a single season. Name them. *Answer on page 119.*

17 From 1986 through 1995 the Mets' television announcers remained the same, with one or two additions along the way. For the most part, however, it was made up of four ex–major leaguers who combined in their careers to pound 778 home runs, drive in 3,267 runs, and make fourteen All-Star teams along the way. Name the quartet. *Answer on page 121.*

18. See if you can match these Mets with the managers they broke into the league playing for:

1. Tom Seaver	A: George Bamberger
2. Jon Matlack	B: Gil Hodges
3. David Wright	C: Joe Torre
4. Darryl Strawberry	D: Wes Westrum
5. Wally Backman	E: Art Howe

Answer on page 123.

19. Mets pitcher Matt Harvey had a major-league debut to remember when he broke into the league in 2012. He set a franchise record by striking out 11 batters in his first game and became the first pitcher since 1900 to strike out 10 or more batters in his first-ever game. He also stroked a double to record his first big-league hit. Oh yeah, he did all of this in five and a third innings. The question is, what team did he do this against? *Answer on page 125.*

20. OK, here we go—it's time for Round Three of Name Those Mets. The first two editions of this game were not all that hard. However, they were both for Mets fans who are a little bit older. This one is going to be up your alley if you are a big fan of the 2016 Mets. Here we go:

CLUE #1: They both played third base for the Mets in 2016.

CLUE #2: If one of their moms named us the other's first name, they would have one of the strangest names ever in baseball.

CLUE #3: One of them has logged 1,399 career regular season games and one of them has logged just 39 regular season games.

CLUE #4: Although they both played third base for the Mets in 2016, one of them has started five games at the hot corner and the other has made his living mostly as a second baseman.

CLUE #5: One of the players has played in the post-season with four different franchises. The other one has only appeared in the postseason just once, registering one at-bat.

OK, now it's all you—Name Those Mets!
Answer on page 125.

ALL-STAR LEVEL — ANSWERS

1 The answer to this question is easy—but only if you can span the generations of Mets history. Oh, and you need to know who was on the mound for each of the championships.

The second championship—in 1986—might be an easier answer for most. After all, the photo of Jesse Orosco falling to his knees and reaching for the heavens is probably one of the most recognizable images in franchise history. But how did Orosco get to the Mets? Who was traded for him that would have been on the mound for the Mets' only other championship? Nolan Ryan is a good answer. He had a win and a save in his two postseason appearances in 1969 and was traded several years later. However, Nolan Ryan is not the correct answer.

In 1969, the Mets had thoroughbreds as starting pitchers, and going to the bullpen to close out a game—let alone a World Series—was not a given. Then there is the age difference. Those two World Series were seventeen years apart.

The answer is Jerry Koosman, who was traded to the Minnesota Twins following the 1978 season for minor-league pitcher Greg Field and a player to be named later. That player to be named later was named Jesse Orosco, who was drafted by the Twins in the second round of the January 1978 amateur draft. After an up-and-down start with the Mets, Orosco became an important part of the Mets' bullpen by 1983. By 1986, Orosco and teammate Roger McDowell were a formidable one-two or two-one punch, depending on the game situation. It was Orosco the lefty and McDowell the righty. When the call came to close out games in the 1986 playoffs, that call went to Orosco.

More than a week after an exciting National League Championship Series, where Orosco slammed the door on the Houston Astros in a Game Six marathon, he was once again on the mound at the end of a game—and a World Series. Two nights after the now legendary Game Six of Mookie–Buckner fame, Orosco climbed the mound to finally put an end to things—and give the Mets their second world title.

One Mets fan, far away from Shea Stadium that night, recalls sitting at home with a big smile on his face. "That's great, two good left-handers," Koosman said with a hearty laugh. "I was happy for Jesse, he carried on the energy. It's amazing how things turn out looking back in history."

2 This is one of the tough ones, because Gooden actually has never been officially listed as having a uniform number other than his Number 16. However, in spring training of 1984, before his first major-league season, Gooden wore Number 64—paying homage to the year he was born.

In a 1985 baseball card set, distributed by the Woolworth's department store, Gooden is depicted wearing a number 64 jersey.

Gooden reprised his role in number 64 prior to the 1993 season, when he once again donned a jersey with the

Dwight Gooden, always known as number 16 for the Mets, donned the number 64 in his first spring training. *Photo of Topps® Trading Cards used courtesy of The Topps Company, Inc.*

same number he wore before he pitched in the majors. However, Gooden never appeared in a game as a member of the Mets in anything other than number 16.

He did, however, wear both 11 and 17 during his two stints with the Yankees. But Mets fans have purged those images from their memories, so the numbers Gooden wore while in pinstripes are hardly relevant.

As an aside, Gooden did wear number 00 as a Met for a short time during spring training in 1989. That, however, was more of a joke than anything else and didn't last long.

3 Yo Mama! No, seriously, it was Yo's mama. Yoenis Cespedes that is.

Cespedes's mother, Estela Milanes, was a pitcher for the Cuban Olympic team in 2000. Her fastball was clocked as fast as 80 miles per hour.

When Cespedes first arrived in New York in 2015, he was known for throwing the ball back from the outfield underhand, ala a softball pitcher. While Cespedes admits his mother didn't teach him to throw that way, he did acknowledge to reporters that it was "sort of in my blood."

Luckily for Mets fans, Cespedes has a whole lot of blue and orange in that blood, as well.

After signing a three-year contract with the Mets prior to the 2016 season, the slugger opted out of the deal following the season, making him the highest-profile free agent on the market. Cespedes wasn't on that market all that long, however, signing an iron-clad, four-year deal in late November. The $110 million contract—which

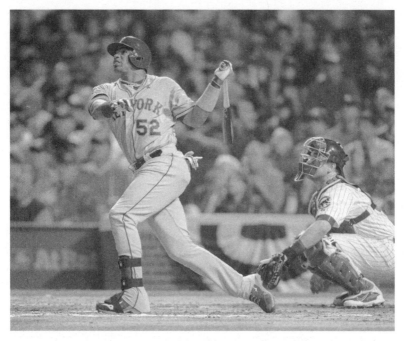

Yoenis Cespedes was born with baseball in his blood. *Photo courtesy of the National Baseball Hall of Fame Library.*

ensures the slugger will call Citi Field home through the 2020 season—made Cespedes one of the richest men in baseball and was the largest free-agent deal in team history.

It was not hard to justify Cespedes's value to the Mets, given that he helped lead the team to the postseason for two straight seasons. Thanks to his ferocious 57 games with the Mets in 2015, a stretch during which he pounded out 17 home runs and drove in 44 runs, New York won the National League pennant for the first time since 2000. Cespedes then followed up his 2015 performance by hitting 31 home runs and winning his first career Silver Slugger, propelling the Mets to a wild-card berth in 2016.

After Cespedes signed the four-year contract with the Mets, his teammates took to social media expressing their feelings about the deal. "The King Returns," tweeted pitcher Noah Syndergaard; "Happy faces all around. Cespedes for President—four more years," tweeted Jose Reyes; however, reliever Josh Smoker might have said it best—echoing the thoughts of almost every Mets fan— "Yooooo!!!!" he tweeted.

4 Tom Seaver had the worst season of his career in 1982 with the Cincinnati Reds, winning just five times and losing thirteen. It was the only time to that point that Seaver had a losing record, and the Reds decided they no longer needed the one-time ace. So in December of 1982, Cincinnati shipped Seaver back to the team with which he had his greatest success.

When Opening Day rolled around for the start of the 1983 season, there was little doubt who would get the start. With a starting pitching staff of Mike Torrez, Ed Lynch, Walt Terrell, and Craig Sawn, the thirty-eight-year-old Seaver—even toward the end of his career—would start against Steve Carlton and the Philadelphia Phillies.

Seaver pitched well in the opener, in front of 46,687 fans at Big Shea, throwing six scoreless innings and scattering only three hits. However, the Mets did not give Seaver any run support—a problem he would have often in 1983—and the former ace had to settle for a no-decision.

Manager George Bamberger turned to a young pitcher named Doug Sisk to come out of the bullpen and take over for Seaver. Sisk allowed only two hits in his three innings of work, and after the Mets scratched out two runs against Carlton, Sisk was on the long side of the decision. Unlike in today's game, where a closer would be called in to finish off the game, Sisk finished things off by himself. The twenty-five-year-old allowed two baserunners in the ninth inning before shutting the door for good and securing the victory. It was the first of five victories for Sisk in 1983, and was by far the most exciting.

After recording the win, Sisk admitted to the gathering press corps that he never intended to get the call from his manager to replace Tom Terrific.

"George better have a beer, and think about it some more," Sisk joked with reporters after the game. "My scenario called for Tom Seaver to pitch seven good innings, then for Neil Allen or Jesse Orosco to come in and finish. I had no idea I'd even be used."

However, Sisk was up to the task, striking out three Phillies, including Tony Perez, to end the game.

5 The First-Year Player Draft was started in baseball in 1965, and since that year the Mets have had the number one overall pick five times.

The first time the Mets had the opportunity to select first overall was in 1966, and they selected catcher Steve Chilcott out of Antelope Valley High School in California. Unfortunately, the scouts did not really hit a home run on this pick. Chilcott injured his shoulder early in his minor-league career and never made it beyond Double-A. Injuries became commonplace for Chilcott and he was out of baseball as a player by 1972. He holds the unflattering distinction of being one of only two No. 1 picks to never appear in a major-league game. The other was Brien Taylor, who was drafted first overall by the Yankees in 1991.

The Mets had better judgment with their second No. 1 pick, when in 1968 they selected shortstop Tim Foli out of Notre Dame High School in California. Unfortunately, while Foli ended up having a productive 16-year career, much of that was spent with other ballclubs. However, it was Foli who helped the Mets land one of their best—and most popular—players of all time.

In April of 1972, the Mets sent Foli, Mike Jorgensen, and Ken Singleton to the Montreal Expos for Rusty Staub. Of course, Staub went on to be one of the greatest hitters in Mets history. Foli, meanwhile, became a starter for the Expos for the next several years. The Mets would reacquire Foli later in the decade for parts of two seasons, but in the end, he would be remembered as the top pick who helped the team land Staub.

Eight years later, the Mets once again selected No. 1 overall and this time, there was no doubt about their pick. This player was not going to be stuck in the minors for very long and he certainly wasn't going to be packaged in any deal for anyone. In 1980, the Mets used their top pick to take Darryl Strawberry out of Crenshaw High School in Los Angeles.

Strawberry was immediately one of the most impressive players the Mets had ever had on their roster. He was referred to by scouts as the "Black Ted Williams."

After winning the National League Rookie of the Year in 1983, Strawberry went on to have seven All-Star seasons for the Mets. Of course, he was a key piece in the 1986 world championship team, but it was the two following years when Strawberry exploded offensively. In 1987, he slammed 39 home runs and drove in 104 runs. He also stole 36 bases, making him only the second Mets player to ever reach the 30-30 club. His teammate, Howard Johnson, had become the first to join the club earlier in the season.

In all, Strawberry averaged more than 31 home runs per year for his eight seasons with the Mets and will always be known as one of the greatest pure hitters in franchise history. He was, to say the least, a good top pick.

Not so much can be said for the Mets' next No. 1 overall pick, which came in 1984. That year, the Mets picked a young player out of Mechanicsburg, Pennsylvania, by the name of Shawn Abner. While Abner did eventually play in the majors for parts of six seasons, he never appeared in a game as a member of the Mets. Just two years after being drafted by the Mets, Abner was part of the eight-player deal with the San Diego Padres that sent Kevin McReynolds to the Mets. So while Shawn Abner was certainly a bust as a player, he did help the Mets land a key piece of their roster for the late 1980s.

Unfortunately, the fifth and final player on this list is also a member of the "what could have been" club. In 1994, the Mets selected Paul Wilson out of Florida State University with the top overall pick. It was a no-brainer, Wilson reminded people of Tom Seaver and, alongside fellow young pitchers Bill Pulsipher and Jason Isringhausen, was the ace. The trio had been named "Generation K" before accomplishing anything on the field.

After a good start in the minor leagues, Wilson was promoted to the Mets in 1996. However, he hurt his shoulder early in the season and his career with the Mets was over—just like that. Four years later, Wilson made a comeback and pitched for the Tampa Bay Devil Rays and Cincinnati Reds. In the end, Wilson retired with a record of 40 wins and 58 losses. It was a sad ending to a much-hyped career.

Perhaps it's better if the Mets don't select first overall.

6 When Joe Torre was traded to the Mets prior to the 1975 season, he was extremely optimistic. The Mets, just two years removed from the National League pennant, and Torre, just two years removed from being an All-Star, seemed like a good fit. The Mets still had Tom Seaver and solid players like Rusty Staub and Millan.

One of Millan's best days in 1975, however, etched Torre in the record books in a way he would rather forget. On July 21, the Mets played their 90th game of the season—a contest against the Houston Astros. Millan could do no wrong, going 4-for-4 at the plate, all singles. He was doing a great job of setting the table for Torre. Torre, however, clearly wasn't hungry.

The nine-time All-Star and former National League Most Valuable Player promptly grounded into four double plays, for which he blamed Millan—of course, sarcastically.

"I'd like to thank Felix Millan for making all of this possible," Torre said, tongue in cheek, to reporters after the game. "He ought to get an assist."

For Millan's part, he was still laughing about Torre's performance—and postgame comments about it being his fault—four decades later when he was interviewed by the *New York Daily News*.

"He could've hit a home run or something, couldn't he?" Millan joked.

7 The answer to this question actually sparks so many more questions. The first being—how is Bartolo Colon the answer to any hitting question?! But there you have it, starting pitcher Bartolo Colon—at the age of forty-two—became the oldest major leaguer to hit the first home run of his career.

Debuting in 1997 with the Cleveland Indians, he spent the majority of his career in the American League—hardly ever holding a bat. In fact, in his rookie season, he had only one plate appearance, striking out.

For the first five and a half years of his career, Colon was relegated to 28 interleague at-bats while with the Indians. During that time, he had only four hits—a .143 batting average. Not all that unusual for a starting pitcher in the American League.

After a half of a season with the Montreal Expos in 2002, where he went 5-for-39 (.128), Colon was traded back to the American League, where he spent the next ten seasons. Over that entire stretch, Colon had 29 at-bats—with one base hit.

Things changed for Colon's hitting fortunes when he signed with the Mets—although at the time he had no idea how much those fortunes would actually change. In fact, when he first signed in 2014, Colon's hitting was the punchline for many—including Colon himself.

After all, this is a man who had one hit over the past ten seasons. So when he went 2-for-62 in 2014 (.032), no one was all that surprised. In fact, fans seemed to get more of a kick out of Colon's at-bats, as his helmet often fell off when he let his powerful swing rip.

Prior to the 2015 season, the Mets hired Kevin Long as their new hitting coach. Long assured Colon that he would make him a better hitter. It was probably the hardest project of Long's career—and maybe of Colon's career, as well. Sure enough, as the Mets were making their way through a pennant-winning season, Colon's hitting greatly improved.

The pitcher, affectionately known as Big Sexy, had his way with a number of pitchers during the 2015 campaign, going 8-for-58, with a double and four runs batted in. While Colon was not in line to be the Silver Slugger among pitchers in the National League, he did hit .138—the best batting average of his career by far.

Colon, however, saved his biggest at-bat for the 2016 season—against San Diego Padres starting pitcher James

Shields. "Big Game James," as Shields had come to be known, threw a one-ball, one-strike fastball to Colon, who turned on the pitch and drove it over the left-field fence at Petco Park.

"Bartolo has done it—the impossible has happened," shouted Mets play-by-play man Gary Cohen on PIX11.

The team then all left the dugout, ensuring that when Colon made it around the bases he would be alone in there. After a few seconds, with Colon in the dugout smiling by himself, they swarmed him with high-fives and hugs.

While Colon's ball might have left the playing field in a hurry, his trek around the bases was anything but fast. In fact, it took 30.6 seconds.

"He's taking the slowest home run trot you've ever seen," said Howie Rose on WOR Radio.

For Colon, it was a huge accomplishment to go along with his 230-plus victories on the mound.

"It means a lot," Colon said through an interpreter to reporters after the game. "It's something that I still can't believe until now."

8 When Gary Sheffield became the twenty-fifth player in Major League Baseball history to join the 500 home run club, he accomplished a lot more than hitting an epic clout.

Sheffield, who had joined the Mets on April 5, 2009, needed just one home run to move from a prolific home-run hitter to a legendary slugger. The difference between 499 home runs and 500 home runs is so much more than one ball clearing the fence. It seemed unlikely, however, that Sheffield would accomplish the milestone twelve days later, when he was riding the bench against the Milwaukee Brewers—the team he broke in with twenty-one years earlier. After all, Sheffield had not hit a pinch-hit homer in fifteen years. His last, in fact, was in 1994 as a member of the Florida Marlins. To pile up more things going against him, none of the previous twenty-four men to join the 500 club had done so as a pinch-hitter. Oh, one more thing, none of them had ever hit his 500th home run with a new ballclub.

So much for history.

With the Mets trailing by a run in the bottom of the seventh inning, Sheffield came off the bench to face Milwaukee reliever Mitch Stetter. Nine pitches into the at-bat, Sheffield became the first pinch hitter to make his first home run with a new team punch his ticket into the most elite of sluggers' clubs. The player, who throughout his career was rarely at a loss for words, was admittedly surprised.

"I never thought it was going to happen like this," Sheffield told reporters after the game. "Now I can say 'I'm in the club.' And it's like your degree; no one can ever take that away from you."

Sheffield was extremely grateful to the Mets, who picked him up after the forty-year-old was released by the Detroit Tigers before the season began.

"There was a bigger reason and a higher purpose, and especially being released and coming back to New York and doing it," Sheffield told reporters, referring to the three seasons when he hit more than 70 home runs for the Yankees. "I knew there was a bigger reason, and I had to keep that in mind."

9 To understand the irony of Gary Carter's walk-off home run in his first game as a Met, you have to look deeper than who he hit that home run against.

First, you have to realize that Carter would have never had the opportunity to be the hero of the day if it hadn't been for another of the team's veteran stars. Not George Foster, who went 2-for-5 with an RBI and two runs scored. He doesn't really fit in to the picture here. However, first baseman Keith Hernandez does.

Hernandez, who was beginning his second full season with the Mets, had a huge day at the plate, going 3-for-5 with two runs batted in. He also drew a walk, reaching base in four of his six plate appearances.

Had Hernandez not been traded to the Mets in 1983, however, it's likely that Carter would not have ended things for the Mets on Opening Day, 1985. That's because the pitcher Carter victimized with his game-winning blast was Neil Allen—the former Mets closer who was sent to St. Louis in exchange for Hernandez.

Allen was a solid reliever for the Mets in 1980, 1981, and 1982, compiling 59 saves over the three-year period. After joining the Cardinals, he moved into their rotation, starting 18 of the 25 games he appeared in.

Neil Allen was a solid reliever for the Mets before being traded to St. Louis for Keith Hernandez. *Photo courtesy of the National Baseball Hall of Fame Library*.

By 1984, the Cardinals had returned Allen to where he belonged—the bullpen—although he served as a setup man for top closer Bruce Sutter. Allen wasn't the closer in 1985 either, but was called upon at the end of the opener against the Mets.

In the bottom of the 10th inning, with the game tied at five, Allen began his second inning of relief work. To keep the irony rich, Hernandez actually led off the inning. Had he launched a home run against Allen, Cardinals manager Whitey Herzog might have imploded. Herzog was safe, however, as Allen struck out his former first baseman. However, his luck ran out with the next batter.

Carter got ahold of one of Allen's curveballs and sent a laser-beam line drive into the Cardinals' bullpen. Game over. "Welcome to New York, Gary Carter," announcer Steve Zabriskie proclaimed over WOR-TV.

10 No, the answer is not Daniel Murphy. Yes, Murphy hit a home run in six consecutive games as a Met—but that was in the postseason. A tremendous accomplishment, indeed, but not the correct answer to this question. That honor goes to a man who played only 86 total games for the Mets—all during the 2004 season—and someone who at one point of his career hit more than 40 homers in a season. However, by 2004, hitting more than 40 home runs in a season was a distant memory for Richard Hidalgo. Still, Hidalgo made the most of his time with the Mets, especially in the power department. Five of the slugger's 21 homers came in consecutive games to set a franchise record.

Hidalgo, who joined the Mets in a trade from the Houston Astros in June of 2004, gave the Mets a respected bat in their lineup to go along with players like Mike Piazza and Cliff Floyd. However, his long-ball streak started on July 1 against the Cincinnati Reds and reliever Mike Matthews. With the Mets leading, 5–0, in the top of the eighth inning, Hidalgo got a hold of a Matthews pitch and sent it deep over the left-center field fence. Not a huge surprise, considering the home-run prowess Hidalgo possessed.

The following night, Hidalgo and the Mets opened up a series against the first-place New York Yankees at Shea Stadium. In the opener, the Mets jumped all over Yankees pitching, jumping out to a quick 5–0 lead after two innings. Then, in the bottom of the fifth inning, Hidalgo ripped a Mike Mussina pitch for a two-run homer and the Mets had a 7–0 lead. It was two home runs in as many games for Hidalgo.

The second game of the series was a slugfest between the two New York teams. In the bottom of the sixth inning, with the Mets trailing 8–6, Hidalgo brought the Mets within a single run of the Yankees when he turned around a pitch from Jose Contreras. The Mets went on to win the ballgame, 10–9, and Hidalgo had homered in three straight games.

The Mets completed a three-game sweep of the Yankees with Hidalgo breaking a 4–4 tie in the bottom of the seventh inning of a game the Mets would win, 6–5. The slugger ripped his fourth homer in as many games to tie a team record when he took Felix Heredia deep.

"I'm just focusing on every pitch," Hidalgo told reporters after tying the club mark. "This is as good a stretch as I've ever been in. . . . I'm so happy to be here, just coming to the park every day makes me feel good."

The following night, the Mets travelled two hours down the Jersey Turnpike to Philadelphia, but the change of scenery did not cool down the red-hot Hidalgo. In the top of the first inning, Cliff Floyd smacked a two-run home run against Phillies starter Paul Abbott. The next batter was Hidalgo, who followed Floyd's blast with a record-setting homer of his own.

11 The Mets had been searching for the franchise's first career no-hitter for so long, most diehards figured it was something that was just never going to happen. Several times, a Mets pitcher had come seemingly within an inch of making history. In fact, there were two times in particular, and it depends on your age to determine which one you remember most.

Of course, there was Tom Seaver, who came closer than anyone in 1969. For Seaver, it wasn't just the Mets' first no-hitter, it was pure perfection. On July 9, Seaver took a perfect game into the ninth inning against the Chicago Cubs at Shea Stadium. After retiring the first batter, Seaver was just two outs away. That is when Jimmy Qualls etched his name into Mets lore. His line drive into left-center field fell to the grass, and so too did Seaver's chance at perfection. It was one of five one-hitters Seaver would throw as a member of the Mets.

Fifteen years later, many Mets fans remember a rookie by the name of Dwight Gooden, who entered the eighth inning no-hitting the Pittsburgh Pirates. However, a lead-off single by the Pirates' Doug Frobel ended Gooden's chance at being the first Met to reach the finish line. Four years later, in 1988, Gooden reached the eighth inning again with a no-no intact, only to lose it when Damon Berryhill of the Chicago Cubs led off the inning with a single.

Not ironically, those two are among the list of the seven pitchers to hurl a no-hitter after leaving Flushing. Seaver threw his no-hitter as a member of the Cincinnati Reds in 1978 and Gooden got his no-no as a member of the New York Yankees in 1996. Seeing those two pitchers, in particular, celebrate their no-hitters may have been harder than watching the other five men on the list.

When Nolan Ryan was traded by the Mets, it was upsetting to both him and the fans. However, it is safe to say that few fans—and even Ryan himself—could have truly foreseen what Ryan would go on to become after being traded to the California Angels in 1972. One year later, he pitched his first two no hitters—the first two of an incredible *seven* no-hitters. Ryan threw one no-hitter in 1974 and one in 1975. Prior to the 1980 season, the fireballer signed with the Houston Astros and promptly threw his fifth no-hitter one year later. In 1990, as a member of the Texas Rangers, Ryan threw an incredible sixth no-hitter, just a few weeks before winning his 300th career game. One year later, he threw his record-setting seventh no-hitter—at the age of forty-four.

Mike Scott was a rather nondescript pitcher for the Mets from 1979 to 1982. In December of 1982, the Mets traded Scott to the Houston Astros for an outfielder by the name of Danny Heep. Not a transaction that was thought of as a big-time trade. However, while Heep served as an extra outfielder and better-than-average pinch-hitter for the Mets, Scott meant everything to the Astros' franchise.

After posting a 15–17 record over his first two seasons in Houston, Scott exploded on the scene as one of the best pitchers in baseball in 1985. That season, the right-hander won 18 games. However, it was just the appetizer for Scott and the Astros. In 1986, Scott once again won 18 games, led the National League with an earned-run average of 2.22 and 306 strikeouts. He would go on to make his first All-Star team, win the National League Cy Young Award, and lead his team to the National League West division title. Oh yeah, on the day that the Astros clinched the division, Scott pitched his no-hitter.

Since sports would be nothing without extreme irony, Scott's Astros would face his former team—the Mets—in the 1986 National League Championship Series. Scott would end up winning Most Valuable Player honors in that playoff series, but as everyone reading this book knows, he would do so in a losing fashion.

The second player on this list to pitch his no-hitter for the Yankees is David Cone, but Cone took it one step further—he pitched a perfect game. It took place in July of 1999, seven years and four transactions since he had left the Mets. Cone was masterful against the Montreal Expos, never going as far as three balls to any batter. When the final Expos hitter, Orlando Cabrera, popped out to third base, Cone—who went 20–3 in 1988 for the Mets—dropped to his knees and grabbed his head with both arms. For Mets fans, they too probably grabbed their head with both arms, saying to themselves, "Oh no, not again."

In 2001, when Hideo Nomo pitched his second-career no hitter, not too many people looked at it as a former Mets pitcher throwing a no-no. But in fact Nomo did pitch for the Mets in 1998, making him a legitimate answer to this question. He accomplished his goal in April of 2001 as a member of the Boston Red Sox. His no-hitter made him just the fourth player in history to throw a no-hitter in both the American and National leagues.

The final player on the list is another one of those moments of irony for the Mets and their fans. Philip Humber was drafted by the Mets with the third overall pick of the 2004 amateur draft. The young pitcher, who had played for Rice University, was named as one of *Baseball America's* top prospects in the game and was a September call-up with the big club in 2007. So when the Mets started talking to the Minnesota Twins about a trade for ace Johan Santana, it was a given that Humber's name was one of the first to come up. In February of 2008, Humber was one of several players sent to Minnesota for the Cy Young Award winner.

Things did not work out well for Humber in Minnesota and he became a free agent following the 2009 season. After spending one season with the Kansas City Royals, Humber was released following the 2010 season. He signed a free-agent deal with the Chicago White Sox before the 2011 season. It was in April of the 2012 season that Humber had the biggest day of his career. In only his 30th career start, Humber pitched a perfect game against the Seattle Mariners. Mets fans couldn't believe it. Luckily, that feeling only lasted two months. In June of that same season—Santana, the man Humber had been traded for when he was sent packing from New York—indeed pitched the first no-hitter in Mets history. By pitching that one game, Santana erased all of the bad or sore feelings for pitchers on this list.

Through the 2016 season, the San Diego Padres are the only franchise to have never had a pitcher throw a no-hitter.

12 That is actually a true statement, at least in theory. In April of 1960, as New York City moved forward with its plan to build Shea Stadium—even without a team—they announced a feature on the new stadium would have something that no one could have imagined—a retractable roof. The chairman of the Mayor's Special Committee on Baseball announced that the new stadium in Flushing Meadows Park would indeed have a dome covering it in time for Opening Day in 1962. The retractable dome was going to be made of aluminum or lightweight steel and would add about $3.5 million to the stadium costs. Those additional costs would not be the burden of the city nor the team, however. While the team would be responsible for paying the rent for the stadium, the dome costs would be paid for by raising private capital from investors. Until that capital was raised, Shea asked the aluminum and steel companies to allow the city to defer payment on the construction of the dome. According to Shea's initial statement, the chances of the new stadium having a dome were "increasingly strong."

"We would draw all kinds of events there if we get the dome," said Bill Shea, the New York City attorney who was one of the driving forces behind the new stadium. "That would help us pay the rent on the stadium."

Although, he admitted soon thereafter, that the chances were more like 50-50. As time went on, those odds continued to drop and, as we all know by now, there was no roof—retractable or otherwise.

13 There have been many players who have caught for the Mets, but some of the names that you might think would be the answer to this question did not exclusively appear as a catcher for the team. For example, Jerry Grote caught more than any other games for the Mets with 1,176 games behind the dish. But Grote also appeared at third base and in the outfield for the Mets over the course of his career. The catcher who appeared in the second-most games for the Mets is Hall of Famer Mike Piazza with 826. However, Piazza logged 69 games at first base, which rules him out of this question.

In all, the top five members of the list for most games played at catcher for the Mets are not the correct answer to this question. After Grote and Piazza, you have Todd Hundley, John Stearns, and Gary Carter. In fact, you have to get to the sixth man on the list until you have the person who never played another position in his years with the Mets. That man is Ron Hodges, who played in 445 games for the Mets behind the plate and nowhere else. Hodges served primarily as the team's backup from 1973 through 1984. In his 12-year career, he batted .240.

14 Few families have been as prominent in sports announcing—especially in New York—as the Albert family. Sure, there have been father-and-son duos, such as Jack and Joe Buck, and even father-son-grandfather announcers, such as Harry, Skip, and Chip Caray. However, all other broadcasting families fall short of the Alberts.

Oldest brother Marv Albert, who began his career in 1967, broadcast New York Knicks basketball games for thirty-seven years. He has also broadcast for the Nets, Giants, Rangers, Monday Night Football, as well as countless national football, basketball, hockey, and baseball telecasts.

Marv Albert's son, Kenny, is the current radio voice of the Rangers, as well as national telecasts for baseball, football, and hockey. His daughter, Denise, is a reporter for NBA TV.

Marv Albert's younger brother, Al, has been a broadcaster since the 1970s, calling games for the Denver

Nuggets for more than twenty years, before moving on to the Indiana Pacers. He has also done national NBA games and championship boxing matches.

It was Steve Albert, however—the younger brother of Marv and Al—that slipped into the broadcast booth at Shea Stadium alongside of the great Ralph Kiner and Bob Murphy. The youngest Albert brother has gone on to broadcast games for the Nets, New Orleans Hornets, Golden State Warriors, Cleveland Cavaliers, and Phoenix Suns. He has worked for the Islanders, Rangers, Jets, and even a team called the Cleveland Crusaders of the World Hockey Association. Albert got his big chance with the Mets when Nelson—who was an original Met announcer—headed west to take a job with the San Francisco Giants. Not an easy task for a young broadcaster still in his twenties.

"To be completely honest, I wasn't ready for it," Albert admitted. "If I had it to do all over again, I might have made a different choice, but you don't know that at the time. I was too young and didn't have the proper experience or the stories that people like Vin Scully or Ralph Kiner. I just didn't have them yet. It was nobody's fault, I just needed more years in the business before taking on a challenge like that. But it was an opportunity I just couldn't pass up."

The challenge was really three-fold—he was Marv Albert's younger brother, he was replacing an announcer that had been there since the team's birth, and he was broadcasting in the biggest media outlet in the world.

"It was very strange. First you go into it as Marv's brother and then you take over for Lindsey Nelson," Albert said. "But I had to take the opportunity when it came and I tried not to let any of the other stuff get in the way. Plus, you have to be a little crazy to take over for a guy like Lindsey, who was a legend. It wasn't easy."

It didn't help that the Mets were one of the worst teams in baseball at the time.

"I remember doing some games where the stadium was so empty that I could hear the umpire's ball-strike indicator from the press box," Albert quipped. "It was that ugly at times. The good news was that every fan had his or her own vendor and it was easy to find your car after the game."

Through it all, the challenges Albert confronted with his New York gig helped shape the broadcaster he ended up becoming.

"It turned out to be a very good experience," Albert said. "That was just a small chapter in my career. In the long run it was a good thing for me. It made me appreciate the good experiences in my career even more. It made me prepare harder."

15 On August 27, 1992, the Toronto Blue Jays were looking for a pitcher who could solidify their playoff chances. David Cone, who had been with the Mets since 1987, was part of the Mets' starting rotation that included big-time names such as Dwight Gooden, Bret Saberhagen, and Sid Fernandez. However, the Mets were a huge disappointment in 1992 and on August 27, had a record of 56–67, 14 games out of first place.

Cone was sent to the Blue Jays in exchange for a rookie infielder named Jeff Kent and a player to be named later, which turned out to be a young outfield phenom by the name of Ryan Thompson. Unfortunately for the Mets, Kent truly blossomed after he was traded during the 1996 season. As a member of the Mets, Kent averaged 18 home runs and just over 70 runs batted in during his full seasons with New York. By the time he retired, following the 2008 season, Kent had amassed 377 homers and 1,518 runs batted in. In fact, during a nine-year span from 1997 to 2005, Kent drove in more than 100 runs eight times. The Mets enjoyed none of that success.

As for Thompson, who had been billed as a "five-tool" player, things never really worked out. Thompson played parts of four seasons with the Mets, never batting higher than .251. He did show flashes of power, hitting 18 home runs in 98 games in 1994, but overall his career ended as a disappointment.

Cone, meanwhile, went on to win the world championship with the Blue Jays in 1992. He came back to Flushing for one last cup of coffee and finished his career as a member of the Mets in 2003.

16 This one is not as easy as it might seem. Somewhat obvious answers, such as Keith Hernandez and Dave Kingman, are—in fact—not correct. Hernandez drove in as many as 94 runs for the Mets in 1984 and Kingman, who clobbered home runs at a Kong-like pace in 1982, finished one shy of the mark, with 99 runs batted in. Guys like Donn Clendenon, Willie Montanez, and even Lucas Duda drove in more than 90 runs in a season, but failed to reach the century mark.

One of the correct answers is a player who wasn't on the Mets all that long, but was in fact a Hall of Famer. In addition, it just so happened that Eddie Murray drove in 100 runs for one of the worst, and most disappointing, Mets teams of all time. In 1993, for those who have erased it from their memory banks, the Mets won just 59 games, meaning they lost 103. Not since 1967 had a Mets team lost so many games. For Murray, however, 27 homers and 100 runs batted in were just another bullet point for his Cooperstown résumé. It also makes him the first answer to this question.

The second Mets first baseman to drive in at least 100 runs in a single season was John Olerud, who had 102 RBIs in 1997—his first year with the Mets. This answer really wasn't all that difficult, as that season Olerud batted .294 with 22 home runs and 34 doubles. Despite only playing with the Mets for three seasons, Olerud certainly left his mark on the team. He is one of only three first basemen to drive in 100 or more runs in a season for them and his .354 batting average in 1998 stands as the highest ever by any member of the Mets.

The final member of the trio of first basemen to have more than 100 runs batted in actually accomplished the feat twice. That man is Carlos Delgado. In 2006, Delgado crushed 38 home runs and drove in 114 runs for the National League Eastern Division champs. Two years later, in 2008, Delgado once again slammed 38 homers, but this time drove in 115 runs in for the Mets. While it wasn't close to the 145 runs batted in Delgado collected as a member of the Toronto Blue Jays in 2003, his performances in 2006 and 2008 should not be taken lightly. They are among the most impressive offensive outbursts by any Mets first baseman.

17 A couple of these guys were probably easy to get for most Mets fans. Ralph Kiner, who was an original Mets announcer from back in 1962, was one of the greatest pure power hitters the game has ever seen. Kiner led the National League in home runs the first seven years of his career. The longtime Pittsburgh Pirates outfielder drove in 100 or more runs for six straight years during his prime. The only thing that actually slowed Kiner was injuries, which limited him to playing for just 10 seasons in the big leagues. His play was so staggering during that time, however—and really it was his first eight years that were off the charts—he was inducted into the Hall of Fame in 1975. After his death in 2014, *The New York Times* said that Kiner's on-field accomplishments were "among the most remarkable in baseball history, featuring a concentrated display of power exhibited by few other sluggers."

Another longtime Mets broadcaster was Tim McCarver, who played for 21 years in the majors. McCarver, who was known as an outstanding defensive catcher and true student of the game, also found time to make two All-Star teams. In 1967, McCarver's best offensive year—playing for the eventual world champion St. Louis Cardinals— he finished second in the Most Valuable Player voting. McCarver's teammate, Orlando Cepeda, won the award unanimously, with McCarver a distant second. He did, however, finish ahead of the likes of Roberto Clemente, Ron Santo, Hank Aaron, and another teammate, Lou Brock. Following the announcement that Cepeda had won the award, sportswriter Joseph Durso of *The New York Times* called McCarver St. Louis's "Number One hitter in the clutch." No small compliment.

The third member of the team was fan favorite Rusty Staub, who retired following the 1985 season and moved right into the broadcast booth. Staub, who became a pinch-hitter extraordinaire in his final years, was one of the top Mets hitters during the early 1970s. In 1975, Staub became the first-ever Mets player to reach the 100 runs batted in mark for a single season. Staub actually had two stints with the Mets—first from 1972 to 1975 and then again from 1981 to 1985. Relegated to a part-time player for his second turn at Shea, Staub made the most of his few opportunities. The supremely cerebral player turned himself into one of the best pinch-hitters in the game. Twenty-four of his 100 career pinch hits came in 1983 alone, when he drove in 25 runs off the bench.

The fourth member of the Mets' announcing booth those years was the least productive during his playing days—Fran Healy. Of the impressive numbers achieved by the four players, Healy only accounted for a total of 20 home runs and 141 runs batted in during his nine-year career. Healy was in the right place at the right time at the end of his career, however, winning the World Series with the Yankees in 1977.

18 Matching games are usually not all that hard, because the answer is literally right in front of you. Still, this one is a little more difficult, which is why it is an All-Star Level question. Here are the answers:

1–D, 2–B, 3–E, 4–A, 5–C

Tom Seaver might have been a tricky one for some fans because he has always been associated so closely with manager Gil Hodges, who led the Mets to the 1969 World Series title. However, when Seaver broke into the league in 1967, his manager was actually Wes Westrum, who had held that position since 1965. However, Westrum would not make it through Seaver's rookie year unscathed. After another very poor season by the Mets, Westrum resigned and was replaced by one of his coaches, Salty Parker, who finished out the 1967 campaign. Hodges was hired that offseason.

Hodges, who is one of two managers—along with Casey Stengel—to have his number retired by the Mets, had already become a legendary figure in Flushing by the time pitcher Jon Matlack broke into the bigs in 1971. After a less than memorable start in his first few games in the majors, the southpaw came in to the 1972 season meaning business. That translated into a 15–10 record, a

2.32 earned-run average, and National League Rookie of the Year honors.

David Wright is remembered by most—at least early in his career—to have played for manager Willie Randolph. However, since he is not one of the options for this answer, it is clearly not Randolph. In July of 2004, Wright made his major league debut in Montreal against the Expos for manager Art Howe. It was a short-lived relationship, as Howe would be fired three months later. Howe had nothing to complain about when it came to Wright, though, as the rookie batted .293 with 14 home runs, 40 runs batted in, and 17 doubles in his first 69 games.

The next two on this list are probably the most challenging, as both Darryl Strawberry and Wally Backman are so heavily linked with manager Davey Johnson, who like Randolph, is not one of the choices. When Strawberry broke into the league in 1983, he blasted 26 homers en route to the National League Rookie of the Year Award. However, all of this could not save manager George Bamberger, who was not around to see much of Strawberry's rookie season. Bamberger resigned in early June of 1983, and was replaced by one of his coaches, Frank Howard.

Backman, on the other hand, actually broke in with the Mets much earlier. The twenty-year-old scrappy infielder made his major league debut in 1980 as a September call-up for manager Joe Torre. In his first-ever at-bat, at Dodger Stadium in Los Angeles, Backman had a run-scoring single against Dave Goltz. Later in the game, Backman would crack a run-scoring double to left field.

It was in fact a September to remember for the young Backman, who batted .323 in his first 27 games.

19 Matt Harvey certainly had a game to remember the first time he stepped onto a major-league mound. His memorable five and a third innings—in which he hit 98 miles per hour with his fastball—came at Chase Field in Phoenix, against the Arizona Diamondbacks.

"I haven't seen ninety-eight out of a starting pitcher in quite some time," Mets manager Terry Collins told reporters after the game. "He's lived up to exactly what everybody's talked about."

For Harvey's part, the young pitcher was ready to get his career in the big leagues going.

"When I was warming up, actually, I looked around and kind of took everything in, and at that moment, I really did believe I was meant to pitch in the big leagues," Harvey told reporters following the game.

20 Name Those Mets! Were you able to guess who these teammates from the 2016 Mets were? In a year that saw eight different players man third base, these two combined to play in twenty-six of those contests. As for the second clue, if Ty Kelly's mother had named him what Kelly Johnson's mom named him, the Mets might have a player named Kelly Kelly. Well, maybe not. So there is your answer, Ty Kelly and Kelly Johnson.

4

EXTRA INNINGS

HALL OF FAME LEVEL

HALL OF FAME LEVEL

The following Hall of Fame Level questions are the toughest of the tough when it comes to Mets trivia. Many of these questions have multi-part answers that require you to actually bleed blue and orange. Are you up to the task? If you're not, put the book down right now. But if you think you might have a chance to get even some of these Hall of Fame Level questions correct, away we go!

1 Through the 2016 season, name the three managers who at one point played for the Mets that managed their teams to a World Series title. *Answer on page 133.*

2 There are two Hall of Fame players who entered Cooperstown as New York Mets—Tom Seaver (1992) and Mike Piazza (2016). However, there are twelve other Hall of Fame players who have played for the Mets at one point in their career. How many can you name? *Not including managers, strictly players! Answer on page 136.*

3 During the 2015 All Star Game, Mets pitcher Jacob deGrom struck out the three batters he faced on just 10 pitches, the first time that was ever done. Name the batters he struck out. *Answer on page 141.*

4 Which Mets batter set a team record for most hits and most runs scored in a single game? Hint: both records were set in the same game. *Answer on page 143.*

5 Who is the only Met to be named MVP of the All Star Game? *Answer on page 146.*

6 Who was the Mets' original head groundskeeper? *Answer on page 147.*

7 Although not officially "retired" by the team, only two players have worn uniform number 24 since Willie Mays retired in 1973. One was Rickey Henderson, who wore the number as a tribute to Mays. Who was the other player? *Answer on page 149.*

8 Which Mets pitcher tied a major-league record by striking out the first eight batters he faced in a game? *Answer on page 150.*

9 Which Mets player was actually traded for himself? Yeah, that really happened. *Answer on page 151.*

10 For one year, in 1979, the Mets had a mascot to go along with Mr. Met. Who—or what—was it? Hint: It walked on four legs. *Answer on page 152.*

11 Who is the only Met to triple three times in a single game? *Answer on page 155.*

12 In 1993, Topps printed its first baseball card with an image of Mike Piazza. The future Hall of Famer was one of four people on the card, which was titled, "Top Prospects: Catchers." In addition to Piazza, the card featured Brook Fordyce of the Mets, Donnie Leshnock of the Yankees, and what other future slugger? Hint: At one point he played for the Mets. *Answer on page 156.*

13 Most Mets fans remember that Joel Youngblood played for—and got hits for—two different teams on the same day in 1982. After stroking a single against the Cubs, Youngblood was traded to the Montreal Expos in the middle of a game by the Mets. Youngblood left the afternoon game at Wrigley Field, and rushed to join his new team, which was playing that night in Philadelphia. Youngblood arrived in time to single late in the game for the Expos. Both of Youngblood's hits on this historic day came against future Hall of Fame pitchers. Name them. *Answer on page 158.*

14 Who started in right field on Opening Day in 1983, drove in the game-winning run, but never played for the Mets, nor any other major-league team, ever again? *Answer on page 159.*

15 What Hall of Fame quarterback was drafted ahead of former Mets star first baseman and current broadcaster, Keith Hernandez? *Answer on page 161.*

16 Which current National League team do the Mets have the highest all-time winning percentage against? Careful with this one. *Answer on page 162.*

17 As we stated earlier, every chapter would end with a Name Those Mets question. However, since this is the final chapter—and we have an ultimate Hall of

Fame question to finish the book on—we are going to make Name Those Mets the penultimate question. Here we go:

CLUE #1: When these two men were teammates, the Mets were not a winning team.

CLUE #2: Each of them was an All-Star during their career.

CLUE #3: Each of them at one point of their career led the league in earned-run average.

CLUE #4: They both had sub-.500 records for the Mets when they were teammates, but they also each had more than 200 wins for their careers.

CLUE #5: After each of these players left the Mets, the next team they played for was the crosstown Yankees.

This is a really tough one, good luck and Name Those Mets! *Answer on page 162.*

18 OK, here is the ultimate Mets trivia question. If you get this correct, you are truly a Mets super-genius. The Mets—in essence—set the wheels in motion to acquire David Wright five years before he was born. Beginning in 1977, a series of nine transactions led the Mets to get their future captain. This is the brainchild of the terrific writer, Ben Lindbergh, who first wrote on *Grantland.com* about each franchise's longest lineage. Here is your ultimate challenge: name the transactions. To get you started—it all began when the Mets traded pitcher Jon Matlack to the Texas Rangers. Good luck! *Answer on page 163.*

HALL OF FAME LEVEL — ANSWERS

1 One of the three managers is a win-win for the Mets and their fans. Everyone remembers that legendary Brooklyn Dodgers first baseman Gil Hodges led the Amazin' Mets to the 1969 world championship, but perhaps not everyone may remember that Hodges played for the Mets.

In 1962, the Mets' first year in existence, Richie Ashburn and Gil Hodges gave them some name recognition.

Hodges was an eight-time All-Star and three-time Gold Glove Award winner for the Brooklyn and Los Angeles Dodgers. He was a very popular player for the loveable Dodgers, and played a key role in Brooklyn's 1955 championship. Hodges also played a huge role in the Los Angeles Dodgers' 1959 title run, batting .391 with nine hits and a homer in the World Series.

Left unprotected at the age of thirty-seven in 1961, he was taken by the Mets in the expansion draft. It was a welcome change for Hodges, who had been relegated to a part-time role by the Dodgers.

"Not playing regularly the past two seasons with the Dodgers kind of got me down," Hodges told reporters after signing his contract with the Mets. "I didn't complain but I certainly wasn't happy about sitting on the bench. It has an effect on my confidence and my timing. Playing all the time, I think, will straighten me out."

As for Hodges's feelings about playing for what appeared to be a very poor roster?

"I don't think this club hasn't a chance," Hodges said. "We have a number of first-division players and if we get pitching, we will have a chance."

They didn't get pitching, and they never had a chance.

However, seven seasons later, Gil Hodges's Mets had plenty of pitching, led by Tom Seaver, Jerry Koosman, and Nolan Ryan. That pitching, along with the some of the timeliest of hitting in the history of the game, led the Mets to the most improbable of world championships. Hodges was, by all accounts, a no-nonsense manager who his players adored.

Unlike during his playing days with the Mets, Hodges inherited a team in 1968 that was starting to be shaped with tremendous talent: Seaver, Koosman, Grote, Ryan, Agee, Swoboda, and others. The pieces were in place and after winning 73 games in 1968, Gil Hodges and his Mets were poised to shock the world in 1969. And that they did.

The second former Mets player to win a world championship—or, actually four in five years—was Joe Torre. Of course, this answer comes much more bitter than bittersweet for Mets fans. Especially when it comes to Torre's fourth and final title. That win came in 2000 against the Mets. Perhaps it was poetic—if not tragic for Mets fans—that the last time Torre was ever carried off of a baseball field was by his Yankees players at Shea Stadium.

Torre, who was a star player for the Braves and Cardinals, was selected to nine All-Star games. His best season was in 1971 while playing for the Cardinals, when he led the National League with 230 hits, a .363 batting average, and 137 runs batted in. His tremendous season earned him NL Most Valuable Player honors.

After the 1974 season, the thirty-four-year-old Torre was traded to the Mets. His acquisition was extremely welcome and he fit in well with the team. Unfortunately, 1975 was a season to forget for Torre and the Mets. Playing in just 114 games, Torre batted .247 and drove in 35 runs. In one game he would like to forget, he grounded into four straight double plays.

As Torre's playing career drained to an end, he was named as the Mets' player-manager after the team fired Joe Frazier in May of 1977. He went on to manage the Mets for five additional seasons, compiling a record of 286–420.

He didn't fare as poorly during his time as manager for the Atlanta Braves and St. Louis Cardinals. However, he only reached the postseason once until the Yankees hired him.

In 1996, his first season managing the Yankees, Torre led them to 92 wins and a World Series title. He would win three more of those titles over the next four seasons and finish his tenure in the Bronx with a record of 1,173 wins and 767 losses. Despite finishing first in two of his three years with the Los Angeles Dodgers, it was his time with the Yankees that propelled Torre into the Hall of Fame.

Finally, there is Bruce Bochy. Considered one of the most talented managers in baseball today, Bochy had a short stint as a Mets catcher in 1982. Bochy only played 17 games for the Mets, but he did hit well for them, batting .306 with a couple of home runs in just 49 at-bats.

Bochy's playing days with the Mets were short-lived, as New York released the young catcher in 1983. While Bochy's playing career never made people turn their heads, his managerial career certainly has.

After managing the San Diego Padres from 1995 to 2006, it is with the San Francisco Giants that Bochy has punched his ticket to Cooperstown. Bochy led the Giants to titles in 2010, 2012, and 2014.

2 This answer most definitely spans generations of Mets fans, as some of the players are from the earliest era of the Mets and others from much more current teams. However, there are in fact twelve players on this list, so here we go:

Richie Ashburn appears earlier as an answer in this book as the first-ever batter for the Mets. He was also the first All-Star for the Mets, being named to the midsummer classic in 1962. Unlike many of the older players on this list that you are about to read about, Ashburn was still performing at a high level in the final season of his career—his one season with the Mets. He batted .306 that year, despite having diminished playing time. Despite his really strong career numbers, Ashburn was not elected into the Hall of Fame in Cooperstown, New York, until 1995.

Willie, Mickey, and the Duke were New York's center-field trio for many years, as Willie Mays, Mickey Mantle, and Duke Snider patrolled center for the New York Giants, New York Yankees, and Brooklyn Dodgers for much of the 1950s. Ironically, two of those guys are on this list. The first is Duke Snider, who played for the Mets in 1963, the franchise's second season. Snider was the Mets' second representative in the All-Star game. He only played for the Mets that one season, however, and was elected into the Hall of Fame in 1980.

Most Mets fans remember that Yogi Berra managed the team in the early 1970s, but some might not remember that he also played for the team. The former Yankees star played in four games for the Mets as a forty-year-old during the 1965 season. They were the final four games of Berra's Hall of Fame career. For the record, Berra had nine plate appearances in those games, singling twice. He was inducted into the Hall of Fame in 1972.

One of Berra's teammates on the 1965 Mets was Warren Spahn, another superstar player that had some of his final days in the big leagues in Flushing. Spahn saw a lot more action that season than Berra did, pitching in 20 games and compiling a 4–12 record for the Mets. However, unlike Berra, Spahn would not retire as a member of the Mets. After New York released the elder statesman in July, Spahn signed with the San Francisco Giants, for whom he pitched the final 16 games of his 21-year career. He was inducted into the Hall of Fame in 1973.

One of the easiest players on this list to guess was most likely the great Willie Mays. Most Mets fans remember that Mays finished his brilliant career a little less brilliantly as a member of the Mets. In 1973, as the Mets were winning the National League pennant, Mays slugged the final six of his 660 career home runs. He was far from the player he once was, however, and Mays retired following the season. He was inducted into the Hall of Fame in 1979.

Now, we come to some of the more modern players on the list. The first one in that group is fireballer Nolan Ryan. Ryan, who went on to toss seven career no-hitters and strike out a record 5,714 batters during his 27-year career. Of course, the first five of those years, Ryan was a member of the Mets, serving as both a starter and reliever. His World Series win as a member of the 1969 Mets would be the only championship Ryan would celebrate. He was inducted into the Hall of Fame in 1999.

Perhaps the most beloved member of this list is Gary Carter, who was known throughout his career as "The Kid." Carter did not play very long for the Mets, which is often forgotten because his time with the team was so successful. In fact, Carter only spent five seasons with the Mets, from 1985 to 1989. Of course, he spent the first 11 seasons of his career with the Montreal Expos. Carter will always be remembered as a true Met, though, making the All-Star team in four of his five years playing in Queens and being named team co-captain with Keith Hernandez from 1988 to 1989. He was inducted into the Mets

Hall of Fame in 2001 and into the Baseball Hall of Fame in 2003.

Unlike Carter, Eddie Murray will never really be considered by anyone as a true Met. Murray played for the Mets during two of their least successful seasons in 1992 and 1993. Despite the team's struggles, Murray had a very productive 1993 with the Mets, hitting 27 home runs and driving in 100 runs. One of the reasons Murray is not remembered all that much as a member of the Mets is that he went on to play for four other teams over the next four years after leaving the team. Still, his numbers were solid during his time in Flushing. He was inducted into the Hall of Fame in 2003.

Rickey Henderson was certainly unlike most other ballplayers. He was supremely talented and always seemed to produce good numbers for all of the teams he played for, despite marching to the beat of his own drum. Henderson was granted permission by the great Willie Mays to wear his uniform number 24 during his time with the Mets. The Mets have never officially retired the number, but other than one unfortunate situation, no one has worn 24. Until 1999, that is, when Henderson stole 37 bases as a forty-year-old. That came just one year after he led the league with 66 steals as a member of the Oakland Athletics. Henderson's stint with the Mets was short, however, as he was released by the team in May of 2000. He would return in more recent years as a coach, however. Henderson—who played for 25 years and nine different teams—was inducted into the Hall of Fame in 2009.

Roberto Alomar is probably one of the most forgotten superstars to play for the Mets. Mostly because his time in New York was futile. After hitting .336 with 20 home runs and 100 runs batted in in 2001 with the Cleveland Indians, the Mets were excited to acquire the veteran second baseman during the offseason. That excitement was never realized, however, as Alomar's production dropped off immediately. In 2002, Alomar's batting average dropped to .266, he hit only 11 homers and drove in just 53 runs. He was traded to the Chicago White Sox midway through the 2003 season. Alomar was inducted into the Hall of Fame in 2011.

Tom Glavine surprised the baseball world when he signed with the Mets after the 2002 season. Glavine had productive years for the Mets from 2003 to 2007, after killing them for years as a member of the Atlanta Braves. He reached the postseason with the Mets in 2006 after a solid 15-win campaign. He won 13 games for the Mets in 2007, including the 300th of his career. However, he will be best remembered by Mets fans for getting shellacked in a must-win game on the last day of the 2007 season. With the Mets needing a win to have a chance to reach the playoffs, Glavine surrendered seven runs while recording just a single out. It was his last appearance as a member of the Mets. He was inducted into the Hall of Fame in 2014.

Finally, we have Pedro Martinez. Pedro quickly became a beloved member of the Mets family, whether he was able to pitch or not. Most of all because he took a chance on becoming a Met when they needed someone to be a face of the team. At the time of his free agency with the Boston Red Sox, his teammate David Ortiz was quoted in the media as saying that there was "no way Pedro was going to no Mets." Well, he did and the Mets could not have been happier. After helping lead the Red Sox to a world championship in 2004, Martinez signed a four-year deal with the Mets. He won 15 games in 2005 with an earned-run average of 2.82, had more than 200 strikeouts, and led the National League with a WHIP of 0.95. Injuries undermined the rest of Martinez's time with the Mets, as he would only win a total of 17 games over the next three seasons. He was inducted into the Hall of Fame in 2015.

3 Mets pitcher Jacob deGrom was simply untouchable on July 15, 2015, at the Major League Baseball All-Star Game, played at Cincinnati's Great American Ballpark. Thirty-one years earlier, Mets rookie pitcher Dwight Gooden—the youngest pitcher ever to appear in an All-Star Game—burst on the national scene, striking out all three batters he faced. In that game, Gooden mowed down Lance Parrish, Chet Lemon, and Alvin Davis. It was a scene that Mets fans of a certain age will always remember—Gooden getting a high-five from his future teammate, then–Montreal catcher Gary Carter.

The next generation of Mets fan saw deGrom one-up Gooden in 2015 when the young hurler struck out three batters on just 10 pitches—an All-Star Game record. The first batter he faced was Stephen Vogt. However, that

Jacob deGrom's performance in the 2015 All-Star Game was truly historic. *Photo courtesy of the National Baseball Hall of Fame Library.*

didn't last very long. Three 97 mile-per-hour fastballs . . . one out. The second batter was Jason Kipnis, who told reporters after the game that facing deGrom's heat was like blunt-force trauma. "It was good morning, good afternoon, ball outside, goodnight," Kipnis said. The last batter deGrom faced—and dominated on three pitches—was Jose Iglesias, who went down not on a fastball but on a nasty 81-mile-per-hour curveball. Following the performance, Mets teammate Zack Wheeler tweeted: "LOL" with two rocket emojis and three flame emojis. "Because I knew I had just one inning, I was just letting it go," deGrom told reporters after the game.

4 One of the greatest—and underrated—ballplayers to ever slip into a New York Mets uniform is most definitely Edgardo Alfonzo. In the late 1990s and early 2000s, Alfonzo was one of the best players in all of baseball.

In 1999, Alfonzo batted .304 for the Mets, with 41 doubles, 27 home runs, and 108 runs batted in. He won the Silver Slugger, as the best-hitting second baseman in the National League, and finished in the top 10 of the Most Valuable Player voting. However, it was on August 30 of that year that Alfonzo etched himself into the Mets record book forever.

In a matchup of playoff contenders, the second-place Mets entered the Astrodome to face the Astros, who were leading the National League Central. The game was over before it started, with the Mets jumping out to a quick 7–0 lead after two innings. Alfonzo got the scoring parade going with a long, one-out home run in the top of the first inning. Thanks to the Mets' hot hitting on this night, Alfonzo would once again come to the plate in the top of the second inning, singling to right field and eventually scoring on a John Olerud double. This was just the start of Alfonzo's night, however.

In the top of the fourth inning, Alfonzo ripped into a pitch from Houston reliever Brian Williams for a two-run home run. By the end of four innings, Alfonzo was

Edgardo Alfonzo doubles in the ninth inning at Houston on August 30, 1999, for his sixth hit of the game. *AP Photo/Brett Coomer.*

already 3-for-3 with two home runs and three runs scored. Two innings later, it became apparent that Alfonzo was having more than just your run-of-the-mill great night when he crushed his third home run of the game—his fourth hit and fourth run scored. Alfonzo would clearly have at least one more at-bat in the game—and possibly more. In the top of the eighth inning, with the Mets leading 12–1, Alfonzo led off the inning with a line-drive single to left field. Later that inning he would later score his sixth run of the game—a Mets record.

Thanks to the fact that the Mets were putting on an offensive display in Houston on this night, Alfonzo would get an incredible sixth at-bat in a nine-inning game.

"I was doing that game with Fran Healy in the Astrodome and we were having a playful little discussion before Alfonzo came up for the last time, because at that point he had three home runs and was five-for-five," said Howie Rose. "We were wondering what would be bigger, if he got the four home runs, or it was just six-for-six. I just remember how locked in he was that day. If any Met of that era was going to get six hits in a game, it was going to be Alfonzo."

Sure enough, Alfonzo got his opportunity in the top of the ninth inning and promptly ripped a double to right field. That completed a 6-for-6 night, the supremely talented Alfonzo scoring six runs along the way.

"You talk about underrated players . . . Edgardo Alfonzo was underrated," Rose said. "He's as good a pure offensive player as [the Mets] have ever developed. You can put Cleon Jones, David Wright, and Edgardo Alfonzo on a very short list of tremendous offensive players that were ever developed by the Mets."

Going 6-for-6 was just one of the many memorable moments Alfonzo provided for Mets fans in what seemed to be a far-too-short career.

"He is, to this day, as classy a player as the Mets have ever had," Rose said. "He was a terrific hitter, he's a solid citizen and boy, you would love to have a couple of more Edgardo Alfonzo's in your system."

While Alfonzo remains the only correct answer to this question, having gone 6-for-6 *and* scoring six runs in a single game, Wilmer Flores did enter half of the conversation in the summer of 2016. On a sunny day in early July, Flores became just the second Met to go 6-for-6 in a game. Alfonzo was so impressed with the feat that he called Flores following the game to congratulate him. For his part, Flores—who hit two home runs and scored three runs in the game—was excited to tie Alfonzo's single-game hit mark.

"It's definitely a good feeling, being part of history," Flores told reporters following the 14–3 victory over the Chicago Cubs.

5 One of the highlights of Jon Matlack's 1975 season was being named to the All-Star team. The fact that he was able to get into the game, pitch well, and be named as the game's co–Most Valuable Player with Bill Madlock of the Cubs was all gravy.

"It was an exciting time and a very special honor to be involved in that game," said Matlack.

The left-hander pitched two scoreless innings for the National League and ended up as the game's winning pitcher. However, the Mets' lone All-Star Game MVP almost never made it out of the bullpen. To make matters worse, he was ready to blame Tom Seaver, his buddy in the Mets' rotation—tongue-in-cheek, of course. With the National League leading 3–0, and Seaver on the mound, Boston's Carl Yastrzemski sent a long blast to right-center field, where Matlack was warming up in the bullpen.

"I was in the bullpen getting myself loosened up and ready and starting to do my warm-up throws," Matlack remembered. "The home run damn near hit me in the head as I was warming up. I heard the bat crack and the guys in the bullpen started yelling, 'Watch out, Watch out' and the ball came flying in."

Fortunately, the ball eluded Matlack. However, he says he definitely would have blamed Seaver had he gotten plunked. "I would have blamed him any chance I could," said Matlack, laughing heartily.

6 It's not that often that a baseball fan thinks about the groundskeepers. However, most Mets fans over a certain age remember Pete Flynn very well. Flynn was the head groundskeeper at Shea Stadium from 1974 through the year it closed in 2008. He also was featured in the Billy Joel documentary *Last Play at Shea*. However, Flynn was actually on the groundskeeping team for more than ten years before taking over as the head groundskeeper. The man who hired him—John McCarthy—was himself a legendary head groundskeeper.

Before taking the job as the Mets' head groundskeeper at the Polo Grounds in 1962, he had already put in more than a decade as the head groundskeeper for the New York Yankees at Yankee Stadium. However, it was at Shea Stadium where McCarthy became a star—just as the Mets' star was rising.

"He absolutely loved being around the ballpark," said his son, Michael McCarthy. "He had two good lines he

Johnny McCarthy was the Mets' original head groundskeeper.
Photo courtesy of Michael McCarthy.

used to use when asked what he did for a living, 'I'm a diamond cutter' or 'I'm outstanding in my own field.'"

McCarthy made his biggest contribution to the Mets and to Shea Stadium following the Mets clinching the National League East in 1969 when the fans literally ripped up the field. When it was all over, Shea was an absolute mess. McCarthy, however, made it all right again.

"There was a picture of him standing on the torn grass on the cover of *The New York Times*, holding his head in his hands as if to say, 'How are we going to fix this!' But of course they did," said McCarthy, who remembers his Dad as a "one of a kind with a great sense of humor and a tireless worker."

McCarthy, who continued to work in the Mets front office until his death in 1994, has a plaque dedicated to him at Citi Field in the grounds crew room. It reads: "John P. McCarthy: An Original Met."

7 When Willie Mays was shoved into retirement following the 1973 season, Mets owner Joan Payson reportedly promised Mays she would never allow number 24 to be worn again by a member of the Mets. Seven years later, however, the number had not been officially retired when the Mets were sold. Still, new ownership appeared to honor the handshake deal that Payson had made with Mays—until 1990.

Toward the end of the summer of 1990, the Mets were struggling and their starting shortstop, Kevin Elster, went down with an injury. Career minor leaguer Kelvin

Torve was called up from Triple A and found a uniform in his locker when he arrived at the ballpark, as any player would expect.

"I just got there and saw a locker with my uni in it, No. 24," Torve recalled in an interview with authors Jon Springer and Matthew Silverman in *Mets By The Numbers*. "I didn't give a second thought to it. I don't know who assigned the number."

Shortly thereafter, Torve was made aware that a mistake had been made and was issued number 39.

"I had spent a long time in the minors. I was just happy to be there," Torve said in *Mets By The Numbers*. "I would have taken two-point-four if they'd asked me to."

Nine years later, with permission from Mays himself, Rickey Henderson wore number 24 with the Mets. He did so again when he returned to the Mets for part of the 2007 season as a coach.

8 Pete Falcone does not hold too many Mets pitching records, but the fact is, Falcone did own this record for more than thirty-four years. In On May 1, 1980, Falcone struck out the first six Philadelphia Phillies he faced. However, as the question states, the current record holder struck out the first *eight* batters to come to the plate. So who knocked Falcone out of the record books? Why, it is the gentleman whose face graces the cover of this very book—Jacob deGrom.

DeGrom, who was marching through his rookie season in 2014 like a thoroughbred, struck out the first eight

Miami Marlins to come to bat on September 15 at Citi Field.

In the top of first inning, the Mets rookie stuck out Christian Yelich swinging to start the game, followed by Donovan Solano—also swinging—and finally, Casey McGehee looking to end the inning. In the top of the second frame, deGrom struck out Marcell Ozuna looking, before recording swinging strikeouts of Justin Bour and Adeiny Hechavarria. Six up, six strikeouts to tie the team record.

In the top of the third inning, deGrom first struck out former Met Jordany Valdespin looking, followed by Jeff Mathis, also looking. That brought up the opposing pitcher, Jarred Cosart, who was new to the National League and taking only his seventeenth major-league at-bat. DeGrom admitted after the game, he was very aware of the situation when Cosart came to the plate.

"I threw ball one, so I thought maybe he'd take the next one," deGrom told reporters. "I threw it right down the middle. I was trying to go outside corner and I just left it over the middle."

Cosart, who acknowledged he had no idea that deGrom had struck out the first eight batters to come to the plate before him, singled to right field.

DeGrom ended up pitching seven innings, striking out 13 Marlins.

9 In April of 1962, the Mets purchased a player by the name of Harry Chiti from the Cleveland Indians. Chiti had broken into the big leagues in 1950, serving mostly as a catcher for the Chicago Cubs and Kansas City Athletics. In 1961, after playing in just five games for the Detroit Tigers, the twenty-eight-year-old was traded to the Baltimore Orioles, who in turn traded him to the Cleveland Indians. However, before ever playing for the Tribe, he was shipped to the Mets.

After playing in just 15 games for the Mets in 1962—and batting under .200—the Mets sent Chiti back to the Indians on June 15 to complete the trade for, yes—in essence—himself.

10 In 1963, Mets fans first got a glimpse of Mr. Met—a baseball-headed man who served as the team mascot. At first, Mr. Met was only an animated character, but in 1964 a real-life Mr. Met began to entertain the fans in the team's new ballpark. However, while Mr. Met is alive and well as the Mets' true mascot, for a brief time he had a little competition.

In 1979 the Mets were a dreadful team and Shea Stadium was in a state of total disrepair. It was a depressing time for the die-hard fans, including a twenty-five-year-old Howie Rose, who of course has gone on to be one of the most respected Mets historians there is.

"Nothing was more depressing than seeing that ballpark and seeing that team in 1979," said Rose. "I know there were worse seasons, but to me that was the low point in the history of the franchise. New York City was broke, Shea Stadium was a municipal building, and it was in ridiculous disrepair for a place that was only fifteen years old. . . . To see the way it looked in 1979 was tremendously depressing. It just hurt."

To make matters worse, the Mets turned to a mule for some luck. An odd choice, to say the least. In 1979, only 788,905 fans—an average of just 9,621 fans per game—passed through the turnstiles at Shea Stadium. However, those who did attend a game in Flushing got the chance to see something truly unique—Mettle the Mule. Mettle would stride up and down the sides of the field before the game, and during the game would be tied just beyond the outfield fence. The mule was the idea of the daughter of Mets owner Lorinda de Roulet and was named Mettle thanks to a contest among the fans.

"Mettle did little for the Mets in 1979 … the team finished in last place," wrote Ken Belson in *The New York Times*, adding that the mule was gone the very next year when the team was sold to Nelson Doubleday and Fred Wilpon. "The new owners wisely chose to send Mettle packing and spend their money on other things."

Ken Belson's brother, Jeff, was a lifelong Mets fan who had a Sunday season ticket plan that fateful season and is responsible for one of the few surviving photos of Mettle.

"I had my camera for that game, and took pictures of Richie Hebner, Lee Mazzilli, Alex Trevino, and Mettle trotting down the line," Jeff Belson recalled. "I thought it was a funny picture at the time and it did sit in my drawer for years until I found the negatives and made copies of them."

Mettle the Mule had a very short tenure as a Mets mascot.
Photo courtesy of Jeff Belson.

Unfortunately, at this particular game—like several he attended in 1979—the sixteen-year-old Belson was forced to fly solo.

"They were so bad, that kids would rarely go with me to the games," he recalled. "My mom thought I was nuts for going by myself, but what the heck, it was a train ride and few bucks for soda, ice cream, and a hot dog in those days."

Thankfully, Belson did go—and take those photos. Otherwise, Mettle might have just gone down in history as a Mets myth.

11 The answer to this question is definitely one of the most unlikely people to ever lead the Mets in any offensive category. By his own admission, Doug Flynn was not known for his bat. However, in 1980—the same season the second baseman won the National League Gold Glove—Flynn set an offensive record that still stands today.

The game was on August 5, 1980, at Olympic Stadium in Montreal. After tripling in his first two at-bats and then grounding out in his third, he stepped up to lead off in the top of the eighth inning. "Believe it or not the third one that I hit was just a routine base hit to left field," Flynn said, "but on the second bounce it hit a seam in the artificial turf and bounced right over the fielder's head."

Flynn had one more opportunity to bat when he came up in the ninth inning.

"I got up to bat and [Montreal catcher] Gary Carter said to me, 'Hey Dougie, you know nobody has ever hit four triples in a game,'" Flynn remembered with a laugh. "I got a fastball right down the middle and hit a one-hopper to shortstop for a double play." A double play that actually ended the game.

Still, it is a record that Flynn will always appreciate—as unlikely as he agrees it is.

"That's kid of weird isn't it," Flynn laughed. "I didn't have speed, but I did have quickness."

Sometime in the early 2000s, Flynn was reminded of his record when it was being threatened by Jose Reyes, who tripled in his first two at-bats of a game.

"All my friends in New York were sending me texts saying, 'Look out, you're record is going to be broken tonight,'" Flynn laughed. "That's what's so great about our sport. The records are there and they are there to be broken."

For Flynn, however, it's been thirty-six years and the record still stands.

12 This is a real toughie, mostly because the fourth person pictured on the card is not remembered as a catcher—at all. However, when Carlos Delgado came up to the majors, he was a catcher. That didn't last too long. Following his two games as a catcher with the Blue Jays, Toronto attempted—unsuccessfully—to convert him into a left fielder. After both catcher and outfield proved to be the wrong spots on the diamond for Delgado, Toronto moved him to first base in 1996, his first full year in the big leagues. Delgado responded by swatting 25 home runs and driving in 92 runs—among his least successful numbers over the next ten seasons. As a member of the Mets—the final four seasons of his career, from 2006 to 2009—Delgado hit 104 home runs, 99 doubles, and drove in 339 runs.

Combined, the three players on that card, number 701 in the 1993 Topps set, slammed 941 home runs and drove in 3,035 career runs—and only three of the four played in the majors. Not too bad for a prospect card.

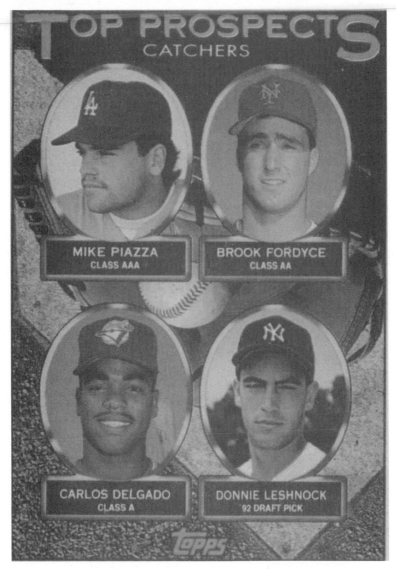

Mike Piazza and Carlos Delgado helped to make this baseball card from 1993 a memorable one. *Photo of Topps® Trading Cards used courtesy of The Topps Company, Inc.*

13 There are so few things that happen in baseball that you can point to that will really never happen again. Sure, it's possible for a player to get hits for two different teams on the same day in two different cities, but highly unlikely. Evidence of this is that it only happened once, and that was more than thirty years ago.

On August 4, 1982, Joel Youngblood woke up as a member of the New York Mets, the team he had played for since 1977. He got dressed and headed to Wrigley Field, where the Mets were scheduled to play an afternoon game against the Cubs. Youngblood arrived at Wrigley to see his name penciled into the third spot in the batting order, against future Hall of Famer Fergie Jenkins. In the top of the third inning, Youngblood cracked a single against Jenkins, driving in two runs and giving the Mets a 3–1 lead. Soon after, manager George Bamberger took Youngblood out of the game.

"He said, 'Joel you've just been traded to the Montreal Expos—they're short players and they'd like you to get to Philadelphia as quickly as you can,'" Youngblood told the *New York Daily News* on the twenty-fifth anniversary of his feat in 2007.

Youngblood then left Wrigley, headed to the airport, and hopped a plane to Philadelphia, where the Expos were scheduled to play a night game. However, something then happened that could have caused this unique milestone to never take place.

"I realized I left my glove at Wrigley Field," Youngblood told the *New York Daily News*. "And I knew that would take away from the time I had and I was jeopardizing my opportunity to make that flight. But I'd played with that glove for years. So I went back, got my glove, and the cab got me to the airport in probably another thirty minutes. It was a 6:05 flight—7:05 Philly time."

Youngblood made the flight and made it to Veterans Stadium, where the game had already started. He entered the game as a defensive replacement in right field in the bottom of the sixth inning. In the top of the seventh, he got his first at-bat for Montreal, and stroked a single to right field against none other than Steve Carlton.

For Youngblood, it was two games for two teams in two cities against two future Hall of Famers. Not a bad day.

14 As mentioned several times in this book, Opening Day in 1983 was a big deal for the Mets and their fans, as it marked the return of the great Tom Seaver. That day, the Mets lineup was a mix of young players such as Mookie Wilson and Hubie Brooks, and veterans such as Dave Kingman and George Foster.

With twenty-one-year-old Darryl Strawberry starting the 1983 season at Tidewater, the Mets needed to find a way to fill the right-field position for a couple of weeks. Most of that playing time would be gobbled up by Danny Heep, who came to the Mets in the offseason in the Mike Scott trade. However, Heep did not get the call for the opener. That honor went to a player by the name of Mike Howard. Having played in a handful of games during the 1981 and 1982 seasons for the Mets, Howard had just 11 hits in 78 plate appearances in his brief major-league career. However, when the pitcher known as "The Franchise" made his return to Shea, it was Howard who was patrolling right field.

Howard's big moment in the game came in the bottom of the seventh inning, when he came to bat against Steve Carlton with the bases loaded. The Phillies brought the infield in to cut off the run at the plate.

"I thought maybe they figured the squeeze was on," Howard told reporters after the game. "So I decided to swing at any fastball that I saw. That's what I got, on the first pitch."

Howard's hit through the left side of the infield gave the Mets a 1–0 lead in a game they would go on to win 2–0. Howard played all nine innings in right field with only one ball hit in his direction. That, as it turned out, did not occur until the top of the eighth inning, when Philadelphia's Bo Diaz singled to right field. That was Howard's only time touching the ball in the field. No fly balls, no line drives, not even an overthrow he had to back up on.

Not unlike the fictional Moonlight Graham from the film *Field of Dreams*, Howard most certainly had to think that he would have other opportunities. Little did he know there would be no other opportunities. When the Mets called up Darryl Strawberry two weeks later, Howard was sent back down to Tidewater of the International League, where he struggled. The Mets had designs on teaching Howard—who was an extremely versatile fielder—to catch. There was even talk of him being the third catcher for the Mets in 1983, but that never happened and Howard never returned to the majors. He is one of only three players since World War II, according to the Elias Sports Bureau, to have his team's season opener be his last major-league game.

15 Keith Hernandez was drafted in the forty-second round of the 1971 amateur draft. The Cardinals made the San Bruno, California, native the 776th overall pick. First-round picks that year included players such as Jim Rice, Frank Tanana, and Rick Rhoden—all solid major leaguers, not to mention one Hall of Famer. The second round had even more glitz, as Hall of Famers George Brett and Mike Schmidt were picked back-to-back with the 29th and 30th picks, respectively. As an aside, Mets pitching coach Dan Warthen was selected ahead of both of those Hall of Famers with the 28th overall pick.

Twelve picks before Hernandez went to St. Louis, the Minnesota Twins selected a shortstop out of South River, New Jersey, with a heck of an arm. However, Joe Theismann found a better way to use that arm than gunning runners out at first base. The same year that the University of Notre Dame quarterback was drafted by the Twins, he was also drafted by the Miami Dolphins. However, contract talks did not work out, and Theismann ended up playing for the Toronto Argonauts of the Canadian Football League for two years. In 1974, however, the Washington Redskins obtained the rights to Theismann. He would go on to play for the Redskins for the next twelve seasons. Along the way, Theismann was selected to two Pro Bowls and was named the National Football

League's Most Valuable Player in 1983. He also led the Washington Redskins to a championship in Super Bowl XVII. Theismann was inducted into the College Football Hall of Fame in 2003. Theismann's decision to play football, clearly, was a good one.

16 OK, you were warned to be careful with this one, and for good reason. The answer to which National League team the Mets have the highest winning percentage is—the Milwaukee Brewers. However, don't forget, the Brewers have only been a National League team since 1998. Prior to that, from 1969 through 1997, they were an American League team. In 1997, the first season of interleague play, the two teams did not meet.

Since joining the National League, through the 2016 season, the Mets have gone 72–55 against the Brewers, for a .567 winning percentage. The Mets have higher winning percentages against seven American League teams, but that is the highest mark over National League teams.

Overall, other than the Brewers, the Mets only have a winning record against three National League teams through the 2016 season—the Arizona Diamondbacks, Colorado Rockies, and Miami Marlins.

17 The final installment of Name Those Mets is a real toughie. Does it make it easier for you to guess if you know that both players are pitchers? Or that they played on the Mets together for only one season—in 1993? During a year where not a single Mets pitcher had a record above

.500, Dwight Gooden and Frank Tanana were among the most successful in the win column. Gooden, who won 12 and lost 15, was actually the best pitcher on the team that season—a season in which the Mets lost 103 games. Tanana, meanwhile, at the end of his long career, won 7 and lost 15. Bret Saberhagen also won seven times for the 1993 Mets, who did not have another pitcher win more than six games that year.

Many Mets fans may remember that after 1994, Gooden's final year with the Mets, he did not play in the majors in 1995. However, when he did return to baseball, Gooden came back with the Yankees in 1996. Tanana, meanwhile, was traded to the Yankees in September of 1993 for pitcher Kenny Greer. Tanana went on to pitch the final three games of his 21-year career for the Yankees. Greer pitched one game for the Mets down the stretch and earned a victory. So in the ultimate of ironies, of the three pitchers—Gooden, Tanana, and Greer—only Greer had an above .500 record for the Mets in 1993. He never pitched for the team again.

18 This is truly an impossible question to answer, but if you get it, you should consider yourself the most elite of all elite Mets trivia players. Here we go—we need to get from Jon Matlack to David Wright:

In December of 1977, the Mets sent starting pitcher Jon Matlack to the Texas Rangers as part of a four-team trade. Among the many players involved in the trade, outfielder Tom Grieve was shipped from Texas to New York. Grieve played for the Mets during the 1978 season, batting .208 in just over 100 at-bats. Following the season, Grieve was traded by the Mets to the St. Louis Cardinals for pitcher—and Brooklyn native—Pete Falcone, who pitched for the Mets for four seasons. Falcone had modest success for the Mets, but playing for the Mets in the years 1979 to 1982, any kind of success was great success. The Mets granted Falcone free agency following the 1982 season. When he signed with the Atlanta Braves on December 20, 1982—the very day that David Wright was born—the Mets received the Braves' first pick in the 1983 draft as compensation. With that pick, the Mets selected Stanley Jefferson, who came up to the Mets in 1986 and played 14 games. That apparently was enough to impress the San Diego Padres, who asked that the Mets include Jefferson in the deal that sent Kevin McReynolds to the Mets. McReynolds, of course, had success with the Mets and was a key piece in the deal to acquire Bret Saberhagen from the Kansas City Royals. At the trading deadline in 1995, Saberhagen was traded to the Colorado Rockies for right-handed pitcher Juan Acevedo and minor leaguer Arnold Gooch—who kept this train running. Gooch made it as high as Double-A Binghamton for the Mets and was part of the Todd Hundley deal that sent Roger Cedeño and Charles Johnson to the Mets. After playing the 1999 season for the Mets, a season during which he stole 66 bases, Cedeño was traded with Octavio Dotel to the Houston Astros for star pitcher Mike Hampton. We are now in the home stretch. Following the 2000 season, Hampton's one and only season with the Mets, he was

The seeds for the Mets getting David Wright were planted before Wright was even born. *Photo courtesy of the National Baseball Hall of Fame Library*.

granted free agency. When the Colorado Rockies signed the ace, the Mets received a supplemental draft pick from the Rockies. With that 38th pick in the 2001 June amateur draft, the Mets selected eighteen-year-old David Wright from Hickory High School in Chesapeake, Virginia.

So there you have it, basically Jon Matlack was traded for David Wright, and you didn't even need a DeLorean. Just an open mind.

Acknowledgments

I never really thought about the possibility of writing a sports trivia book, let alone a book specifically about Mets trivia. I have lived most of my life consumed with Mets trivia, though, so when I was asked by Skyhorse Publishing Editor Julie Ganz to write this book, I was honored. I am thankful to Julie for trusting me with this project and equally thankful to Senior Editor Ken Samelson, whose editing of my manuscript was absolutely tremendous.

Many people helped give this book added flavor, thanks to their personal stories. First and foremost, I would like to thank my good friend Howie Rose, who is a Mets encyclopedia and the best broadcaster in the business. Howie is always extremely generous with his time, and for that I cannot thank him enough. Thank you to former Mets Doug Flynn, Howard Johnson, and Mackey Sasser, and broadcaster Steve Albert, for sharing their wonderful memories with me; and a special thank you to sports executive Mike McCarthy, who shared stories about his father—the legendary head groundskeeper, Johnny McCarthy.

Throughout the research process, I relied on many different newspaper archives and websites for facts and figures, including *The New York Times*, *New York Daily News*, *Newsday*, newyorkmets.com, ESPN.com, MLB.com, baseball-reference.com, baseball-almanac.com, mbtn.net, and grantland.com. As always, I turned to the great John Horne at the National Baseball Hall of Fame Library for his help with photo research, and he didn't let me down. Thanks also to the kind folks at Topps for allowing me to use images of two of their baseball cards. Perhaps the most unique photo in this book is the shot of Mettle the Mule—a one-time Mets mascot. The photo was taken—and saved for all these years—by Jeff Belson. I would like to thank Jeff for allowing me to use the photo, and to his brother, Ken, for writing about Mettle in the first place.

This was really a fun book to write. When you tell people that you are writing a Mets trivia book, they all have questions they want to throw at you. Through it all, I would smile, listen to the questions, and be on my way. Among the Mets diehards who came up with, suggested, or inspired questions for this book are Eric Perli, Sam Oppedisano, Michael Rutter, and Jordan Miller. Thank you, gentlemen, for your terrific contributions. Thank you to Mark Rosenman, a great author in his own right and a good friend. If there were still such thing as a Rolodex, Mark's would be made of gold. I also want to thank Professor Fred Rosen—himself a big-time Mets fan—who more than twenty-five years ago taught me how important it is to write what you are most passionate about.

I want to thank my Mom and Dad for always being there for me in every way; thank you to Ellen, Steve, Melissa, Jason, Derek, Kayla, Abigale, David, Cooper, and Quinn for their unconditional love and support; thank you to Dr. Jean-Marc Juhel and everyone at Buckley Country Day School for all of their positive energy and incredible support; thanks to my son Oliver, who keeps me updated on every scoring change of every Mets game—and my daughter, Lily, who couldn't care less about any scoring change, but has the greatest smile; and finally, to my wife Emily, who at least for a little while doesn't have to hear me insist for the thousandth time that "I must get some writing done tonight."

OK, one last trivia question—two iconic pieces of Shea Stadium survived the ballpark's demise. One was the original home-run apple, which now sits within a flower garden in front of the main entrance at Citi Field. The other is the iconic New York City skyline, which used to sit proudly atop the massive scoreboard in right-center field of Shea Stadium. After the September 11 attacks in 2001, a ribbon was placed over the part of the skyline depicting the Twin Towers. That ribbon still remains on the skyline today, but the question is, where is the skyline? The answer ... it's perched above the concession stands beyond the center-field scoreboard at Citi Field. It may not be Cooperstown, but it is where it belongs—in a spot where all Mets fans can always see it.